MATCHING THE HATCH

MATCHING THE HATCH

A PRACTICAL GUIDE TO IMITATION
OF INSECTS FOUND ON EASTERN AND
WESTERN TROUT WATERS

by ERNEST G. SCHWIEBERT, JR.

Illustrations by the author

Stoeger Publishing Company

Published by Stoeger Publishing Company
55 Ruta Court
South Hackensack, New Jersey 07606

This Stoeger Sportman's Library quality paperback edition is published by arrangement with the Macmillan Company.

Fourth printing, June 1988

Distributed to the book trade and to the sporting goods trade by Stoeger Industries, 55 Ruta Court, South Hackensack, New Jersey 07606

In Canada, distributed to the book trade and to the sporting goods trade by Stoeger Canada, Ltd., Unit 16, 1801 Wentworth Street, Whitby, Ontario L1N 5S4

Printed in the United States of America

DEDICATION

This volume is dedicated to my father,
Dr. Ernest G. Schwiebert, who presented a trout-
fishing outfit to me on my seventh birthday;
and to all the other men with whom I have
fished and loved the great trout streams
of our country.

AUTHOR'S NOTE

THIS BOOK is not entirely a product of my own effort, for I am deeply indebted to many men for the generous help that has been given to me ever since I began the wonderful pastime of fly-fishing for trout. In recalling that assistance, I remember names that cannot be ignored or forgotten.

Mention must be made of my father, Dr. Ernest G. Schwiebert, an historian whose love of trout fishing has been passed on to and carefully nurtured in his son. We still fish together, and without his constant prodding this book might never have been written.

Gratitude must be expressed to Bill Blades, author of *Fishing Flies and Fly Tying,* who started me out properly on that wonderful facet of trout fishing that is fly-tying; to Frank Steel, author of several books on fishing and holder of the first perfect score in the dry-fly accuracy event, for taking *most* of the kinks out of my casting when I was only twelve; to Dr. E. T. Bodenberg of Wittenberg College, who aided me in the identification of the insects collected; to Frank Klune, well-known Colorado angler, who helped to collect many Western species and gave much valuable criticism; to Jeff

Norton, a close angling friend, who gave unfailingly of his time and advice in the preparation of the manuscript; and to the many good friends who fished new flies and offered suggestions in the search for consistently effective patterns.

Many trout fishermen are not too much interested by trout-stream insects. They merely want to get away for a few hours on some stream and catch a few fish. Too often, a few fish is exactly what they catch with such a haphazard approach to trout fishing.

This book was written for the trout fisherman who knows something about the game and is unhappy with his results much of the time. These pages offer refinements to the man who has mastered the fundamentals. Large trout are large only because they have eluded all the natural and man-made hazards that plague them. One must know more than the fish if he wishes to take trout.

I am only an amateur entomologist whose insect knowledge is a by-product of the pursuit of trout. This is not a complete guide to all of our important aquatic insects. It will be many years before all of our leading hatches, like those of the British rivers, have been classified and successfully imitated.

The character of our trout water changes west of the Great Plains, and that portion of our country is treated as Western trout country. Eastern waters are those lying east of the Rockies.

Ours is the grandest sport. It is an intriguing battle of wits between the angler and the trout; and in addition to appreciating the tradition and grace of the game, we play it in the magnificent out-of-doors.

ERNEST G. SCHWIEBERT, JR.

TABLE OF CONTENTS

MAY FLIES IN COLOR

LIST OF DRAWINGS

(Twice Natural Size)

THE EVOLUTION OF FLY-FISHING

THE ARTIFICIAL FLY is quite ancient as a means of fooling trout, for as early as the third century anglers were using flies on the unsuspecting trout of Macedonia. The philosopher Aelian tells us in his *De Natura Animalium* that a fly of wool and hackles was fished effectively on the Astraeus, and that these crude flies were an attempt at matching the hatch.

We know relatively little about the sport of angling in the long years after Aelian, but in 1496, just four years after an historical voyage by one Christopher Columbus, there came from Winchester, England, a treatise on trout flies. Dame Juliana Berners described methods of fly-dressing and fly-fishing in her surprisingly thorough *Treatyse of Fysshynge Wyth an Angle*. Some of those historic patterns are still used today.

In 1653, at the mellow age of sixty years. Izaak Walton published his famous Rich, Marriot edition of *The Compleat Angler* and endeared himself forever to the angling fraternity. This little volume is not just a discourse on fishing methods. It expresses a philosophy of life as well. We know little of Walton's education, but the stature of his angling friends in the intellectual climate of his day indicates that his education must have been adequate, regardless of its nature.

Such men as Sir Henry Wotton, who was an ambassador, scholar, poet and Provost of Eton; John Donne, the well-known poet and preacher, who had no little influence on the thinking of his time; Michael Drayton, who was beloved as England's river poet; and John Hales, scholar and fellow of Eton, were his companions on the stream.

These men fished the quiet British rivers with the long rods and horsehair lines described by Aelian centuries earlier, and it appears that only minor improvements had been made in the tackle used.

In the fifth edition of *The Compleat Angler,* which appeared in 1676, we meet Charles Cotton, who contributed a treatise devoted to the artificial fly and its use. With this work, he firmly established himself as the father of the sport. Although Walton was thirty-seven years his senior, the esteem that these two men had for each other was apparently great. We have tangible evidence of it in their initials over the door of the fishing house along Cotton's trout water in Derbyshire. Cotton was a man of some means, and was later to achieve a reputation as a traveler, scholar, soldier and poet. The little fishing house on the Dove, with its inscription *Piscatoribus sacrum,* is preserved today much as it was in 1674. It stands as a shrine for anglers and has stood through the centuries as visible evidence of the brotherhood existing between them.

Walton and his friends lived in troubled times, for England was torn by war between the Roundheads and the Royalists. Yet the tranquility of the words of Walton gives little hint of the strife. Behind those words is a relaxed spirit born on the quiet pools of his rivers.

Some centuries later, in 1836, we find the serious study of insects creeping into angling, with Alfred Ronalds' classic *The Fly Fisher's Entomology.* It was a book of insects and their imitations, written for the swift rivers in the north of England.

Four years later, John Younger contributed *River Angling* to the literature of fishing. The most significant facet of this work was the speculation on the nymph in the trout diet. Unfortunately, Younger did not pursue his theories, but continued to fish the traditional wet flies instead of exploring nymph fishing.

In the ten years that followed, there appeared two innovations that were to change angling. Edward Fitzgibbon, in the *Handbook of Angling* published in 1847, wrote of British tackle-makers and their exploration of split-bamboo rod construction. Their work was apparently confined to tip sections, and the construction was one of three strips, glued with the power fibers of the cane in the inside of the finished sections.

At the same time, the American gunsmith Samuel Phillippi (or Phillipe) was building rods of split cane with the power fibers on the outside, as we do it today. In all fairness, it must be said that a British rod-maker was also using this method at that time, but Phillippi is credited with inventing the four-strip and six-strip construction techniques. He was a native of Pennsylvania, and his contemporaries verify the fact that he was building split-bamboo rods as early as 1846.

The eyed hook for fly-tying is almost unquestionably of British origin, and we know that it was perfected in 1879 by Henry Hall and George Selwyn Marryatt. It was their work that made the dry fly possible.

To Frederick Halford must go the credit for perfecting the dry-fly technique, and it was Halford who wrote the engaging treatises on the dry fly that aroused American interest in the 1880's. His writings included *Floating Flies and How to Dress Them, Dry Fly Fishing in Theory and Practice, Dry Fly Entomology* and *The Development of the Dry Fly.* Not long before his death in 1914, Halford compiled the dressings for some thirty-odd patterns imitating those insects he had found most important in a lifetime of fishing British trout waters.

Martin Moseley carried on Halford's work in imitating British fly life in his *Dry Fly Fisherman's Entomology.* Much credit must be given to him for this refinement of dry-fly knowledge.

The bulk of the credit for the development of the dry-fly

technique on our streams must go to Theodore Gordon, who is considered the father of the dry fly in America. He was first attracted to the dry-fly method by Halford's *Floating Flies and How to Dress Them* in 1886. The concept of the dry fly must have germinated within Gordon for some time before he took it up, for he once wrote that the dry fly became an obsession with him about the year 1889.

In that year he began to acquire suitable tackle from British firms. His stronger interest may have resulted from the appearance of Halford's second work on the dry-fly technique. Through correspondence with Halford, he obtained a now-famous set of dry-fly patterns, complete with instructions on their tying. Gordon went on to create many of the popular patterns of today.

He spent the closing years of his life pursuing his beloved trout fishing on the Catskill streams of New York. His notes and letters are lovingly gathered for us in *The Complete Fly Fisherman* by John MacDonald. He died at Bradley, near the Neversink, in 1915.

While the evolution of the fly was progressing rapidly, men were learning more of the latent possibilities in split bamboo. Rods were becoming lighter and more efficient under the patient hands of men like Hiram Leonard and the group associated with him. These associates were to form the cadre of fine rod-makers in America, and they included names like Thomas, Payne and Edwards.

During the latter part of the nineteenth century, many figures appeared to contribute to the fly-fishing tradition of this country. Edward Ringwood Hewitt is one to whom we owe much. His writings include *The Handbook of Fly Fishing, Nymph Fly Fishing, Telling on the Trout, Secrets of the Salmon, Better Trout Streams* and *A Trout and Salmon Fisherman for Seventy-Five Years.* His development of nymph techniques for our streams, and his dry-fly innovations, are high among the outstanding contributions to trout lore.

The perfection of the nymph technique is the work of

G. E. M. Skues, the well-known British angler who made the nymph popular. His excellent writings include *Nymph Fishing for Chalk Stream Trout, Minor Tactics of the Chalk Stream* and *The Way of a Trout with a Fly*. There is much excellent theory in these works.

The first American to attempt a correlation between artificial flies and the naturals of our waters appears to have been Louis Rhead, among whose contributions were *The Book of Fish and Fishing* and *American Trout-Stream Insects*. Both of these volumes were published before 1920. Rhead's collections were made largely on the Beaverkill in New York, where the artist-author was a familiar figure. Unfortunately, he used insect names of his own devising, rather than the accepted scientific nomenclature, and his drawings as printed in the finished volumes were far from clear. It is virtually impossible today to identify the species that he collected, and his work has little more than historical interest.

Perhaps the reason that the dry-fly fishing was slow to catch hold in this country lay in the fact that many British writers had expressed the idea that it was a poor technique for fast water. These writers meant that anything much swifter than the placid chalk streams was impractical for the floating fly. Men like Halford were so idolized by our anglers that they did not attempt to use the dry fly on our faster streams.

In 1912, Emlyn Gill published his *Practical Dry Fly Fishing*, which outlined methods of using the floater on our trout waters. Two years later, George M. L. LaBranche contributed *The Dry Fly and Fast Water* to angling literature. He too had been inclined to follow the British dogma and to ignore his own observations as accidental. In a clever piece of writing, LaBranche tells us of the killing of dry-fly trout on the Willowemoc, and how he later shuddered at his heresy. Later success with the floater on fast water stimulated some healthy thought, and his fine book was the inevitable result.

Another excellent angler who contributed no written lore was Richard Robbins of the Beaverkill in New York. Although he did not write, he influenced many of the younger men who frequented that river. According to William Schaldach, in his exquisite *Currents and Eddies,* Robbins was the dean of the Beaverkill in the '20's. He died in 1937 at Roscoe, at the junction of the Beaverkill and the Willowemoc, and is buried in Riverview Cemetery, overlooking the famous Junction Pool. Several seasons ago I spent some time looking for the grave, and was saddened to find that Richard Robbins lies in an unmarked spot above the rivers he loved for so many years.

The spirit of these early anglers lives on today on the Catskill rivers in the nimble, talented hands of Walter and Winifred Dette on the Beaverkill, Harry Darbee on the Willowemoc and Art Flick on the Schoharie. Their fly-tying and fishing have become a legend with the anglers of the Eastern streams; while Jim Deren's Angler's Roost, in New York, has become a headquarters for fine flies, and a gathering place for many of today's enthusiasts.

The work begun by Ronalds in England has been ably pursued here by fly-fishing entomologists like Preston Jennings, in *A Book of Trout Flies;* Charles Wetzel, who wrote *Practical Fly Fishing;* Alvin Grove, with his *Lure and Lore of Trout Fishing;* and Art Flick, in his *Streamside Guide to Naturals and Their Imitations.*

Trout fishing is an art; and like the other arts, it is greatly enhanced by the history and romance that have accumulated over the centuries. The rivers that were the stage for much of this angling drama have something that is lacking on other less-fabled waters.

Rivers like the Beaverkill were the cradle of the dry fly in America, and one cannot fish them without respect for their tradition. With our fishing pressure of today, they can never be what they once were; but even in recent years I have fished the Beaverkill, and have seen the rise at twilight on Barnhart's Pool reminiscent of the old days on the river.

There is something quite wonderful about fishing those storied pools, and one cannot help but feel reverence for the parade of famous rods that has fished before him: Theodore Gordon, John Taintor Foote, Edward Ringwood Hewitt, George M. L. LaBranche, Albert Everett Hendrickson and countless others who have dropped their casts on the pool that gurgles about his waders.

I know that I cannot escape this feeling on the pools away from the highway when the twilight falls and I am alone with the river. One almost expects to round a bend and find the ghost of Richard Robbins, and to be hailed by the old man to tie on a fly for him in the failing light of age and evening.

THE TROUT AND HIS HABITS

WHEN THE AVERAGE FISHERMAN becomes aware of the great tradition and literature that surround the trout with an aura of mystery and charm, he invariably wonders many things about the species that has inspired so much. To many of us, the trout is the aristocrat of game fish, requiring cold, pure water in which to live. Within the lore that has grown around the sport of trout fishing there is a refinement present in no other angling.

Perhaps the greatest charm of the trout is the country in which he abounds. Trout country is synonymous with forests and mountains and white water. The trout fits well into his spectacular habitat, for he is a graceful fish of great beauty. In coloring, the trouts are unrivaled among fresh-water species, from the rich yellow found on the undersides of the brown to the rosy gills and sides of the rainbow. These two forms, with the lovely brook trout, are the principal species found in our streams today. The cutthroat or black-spotted trout, too, retains considerable importance in some of its native Western waters.

The brook trout is known to the biologist as *Salvelinus*

fontinalis, and is thought by many to be the most beautiful member of a colorful family. Technically, the brookie is not a trout, but is a member of a closely related group of fishes called the chars. The chars may be distinguished from the true trout by the presence of only a very few teeth on the vomerine bone in the roof of the mouth. In the chars, these teeth are concentrated in a small area near the front of the mouth. True trout have teeth distributed well along this bone toward the throat.

Originally, the brook trout was found in almost all spring-fed streams from Georgia to Canada. It was a distinctly East-ern and Northern species until stocking spread its habitat to the cold waters of the West. Civilization has brought pollution and lumbering to drive the brook trout from his native haunts, and force him deeper into the wilds. The large trout rivers of the East that still remain are all but devoid of *Salvelinus fontinalis,* which was the only species native to them. Compe-tent men have expressed the belief that the brookie will make his final stand in the back country of the West and the wilds of the North.

The brook trout survives best in waters of sixty-eight de-grees or less that have an abundance of cover and oxygen. Brook trout will die in water that rises above seventy-five de-grees. When the streams begin to get warmer than his pre-ferred sixty-eight degrees, the brookie migrates into the feeder brooks and spring holes along the larger streams.

Like all the trout, the brookie is primarily an insect feeder. He takes about 85 to 90 per cent of his diet in the form of un-derwater insect forms. Brook trout seem to show a marked preference for the immature stages of the caddis fly, an insect order that will be treated later. I once took a large brookie, on the swift Pine in Michigan, that contained sixty-two caddis fly larvae complete with their stick and gravel cases. Number sixty-three turned out to be my caddis fly imitation.

Figures compiled by research biologists in Michigan show that the brook trout is the most susceptible to the wares of the fishermen. In deference to an otherwise noble species, let us say that the brookie is not a stupid fish, but that he has an often fatal curiosity.

The Michigan experiments showed that 40 per cent of the brook trout planted were caught shortly after they had been placed in the stream. An electrical census showed that only 5 per cent remained at the end of the season. The other 55 per cent had apparently succumbed to the rigors of nature.

An inability to stand high water temperatures and a fatal curiosity are the main factors contributing to the decline of the brook trout. Many persons place the blame upon the brown trout, but they should pause to realize that often the brown is the only species able to live in our badly depleted suburban streams.

The brook trout is not a showy fighter when hooked. He uses his strength in an underwater battle that searches out snags and rocky ledges. He is stubborn, and often refuses to give up even after he has been subdued and netted. He is a fish of unsurpassed beauty and a wonderful table delicacy. One cannot ask more.

The rainbow trout is generally considered to be the most spectacular as a fighting fish. His resistance to the hook is high-lighted with threshing leaps and reckless dashes through the heaviest water. *Salmo gairdnerii* was originally a trout of the Pacific slope, but he is now well distributed in our trout streams. The species requires fast water of a relatively high oxygen content.

The unfortunate trait of the rainbow is his intense wanderlust, an instinct born of his Western desire to reach the sea. In Eastern streams where he has been planted, he will leave after attaining any real size and drop downstream until he is stopped by pollution, a lake cold enough to support him, or his beloved salt water. He will return to the streams of his youth in the spring and fall, and is then a great trout from two to twenty pounds in weight. Common inland examples of this migratory trait are seen in the Great Lakes trout rivers,

Catherine Creek feeding Seneca Lake in New York, or the North Fork of the Snake feeding the Island Park Reservoir in Idaho.

Salmo gairdnerii thrives in water with a temperature range of fifty to seventy-five degrees. He can survive in eighty-degree water if it is well aerated. The rainbow was first planted in the East by Seth Green, from the Caledonia, New York, hatchery, in 1874. From that time his distribution in Eastern rivers was rapid, and anglers came to love the California trout for his spirit.

Although he may be taken on the dry fly, the rainbow is primarily a subsurface feeder. Stomach checks indicate that about 85 per cent of his food is taken in underwater life. When he is in the mood for surface food, the rainbow is un-equalled as a sporting fish. He is not so gullible as the brookie, but figures indicate that 45 per cent of the rainbows planted are caught during the succeeding season. Census figures taken at the Pigeon River experimental station in Michigan show that 25 per cent of the rainbows planted will survive through the season.

The rise of the rainbow is an exciting rush when compared to the deliberate rise of the brown, and he is a lusty fish with a passion for white water and the sea. As a fighting trout and a food fish, the rainbow leaves nothing to be desired.

The wary brown trout is not native to the waters of our continent, but was imported from Germany in 1884. The first eggs were hatched at Michigan's Northville hatchery and planted in the Pere Marquette watershed. The brown is not a German fish alone, for he is distributed throughout the trout waters of Europe. The biologist knows him as *Salmo trutta,* and he is the most widely distributed of our trout species.

When the brown trout was first introduced to American streams, he was cordially hated. Irate brook-trout fishermen complained that the new species lacked fight, was not well col-ored, lacked table quality, and was too hard to catch. All of these arguments have proved to be false, and the shyness of the species has saved the fishing on hard-pressed streams. This so-phistication is hereditary, and as one finds him in his Euro-pean chalk streams he may be aptly called educated in all senses of the word.

The brown trout takes about 75 to 85 per cent of his diet under water. This makes him the high-rod dry-fly fish when compared with other species. His liking for surface fare, coupled with the fact that taking him on hard-fished streams is like winning from an accomplished chess-player, makes the brown a deserved favorite with the accomplished angler.

Salmo trutta can stand comparatively warm water, and this makes him the salvation of Eastern trout streams. He can take as much as eighty degrees, but it is likely that he will be found in the spring holes long before that mark is reached. Again, his hereditary qualities make him an ideal fish for waters that can no longer support native brook trout.

Under good natural conditions, the brown grows quite rapidly, and to large size, markedly exceeding the brook in this respect. And unlike the rainbow, whose growth rate is similar to his, the brown is generally not migratory—another point in his favor.

Stream statistics show that 25 per cent of the browns stocked are caught during the following season. Thirty per cent survive. This shows the natural mortality to be relatively low with the brown trout. The same census shows that many large browns are often present in our so-called fished-out streams.

Many of us have come to love the brownie for his sagacity and determined fight. He is a game fish that has saved many trout streams from oblivion. His quiet rise to the dry fly is one of the most satisfying things in trout fishing. He is truly a worthy opponent.

The beautiful Western cutthroat trout is known to the fish-eries biologist as *Salmo clarkii,* and it is much like the Eastern brook trout in its water requirements, feeding habits and fight-ing characteristics. The cutthroat is an excellent fly-fishing trout, but it has a tendency toward a foolish curiosity when in a feeding mood. I have rarely seen real selectivity in this species.

The cutthroat is found less frequently in recent years in waters where it once was numerous, for like the brook trout, the species is not well equipped to cope with warmer waters and heavy pressure from the angling fraternity. The best cutthroat fishing is found in large streams and lakes not easily hurt by fishing pressure, or in the beautiful streams and lakes of the back country.

Although the cutthroat is a fine table fish that rises well to the fly, it is placed in a position of secondary importance in regions where the brown or rainbow trout are found in good numbers.

Many traits of the trout family influence the methods used to catch them. The basic life of the trout can be broken down into five activities: finding suitable temperatures, finding food, resting, eluding enemies and reproducing the species.

Water temperatures affect the trout in two ways: they control both his body temperatures and the amount of oxygen dissolved in the water. The inactivity of trout in warm weather may be directly caused by the lowered oxygen content of the warmer water. Lack of oxygen will result in less activity in any animal.

When the streams get low and warm, the trout will start looking for the spring holes and feeder brooks; apparently they feel better in the colder water. If colder water is not available, they will search out the more broken stretches that gain oxygen from the air. Recent experiments indicate that the presence of excessive carbon dioxide in stiller, warmer water may be a factor in this behavior.

The second important factor in the conduct of the trout is an extremely keen vision. Good vision is essential to survival, for the trout must be able to see his enemies and the insects, many of them tiny, that make up his diet. Most fishermen are well acquainted with the visual powers of the trout. Certain physical laws controlling the transmission of light from air to water affect the ability of the fish to perceive things outside the stream. He sees the world we live in as though he were looking out through a funnel whose apex makes an angle of ninety-seven degrees. Objects that lie outside this cone of refraction cannot be seen by the fish unless they dent the surface film. The surface film outside the visual cone appears to the trout as a gently undulating mirror.

Under water, the trout can see quite well up to distances of about thirty feet. The position of the eyes makes it possible for him to see objects around him in a three-hundred-degree arc. He has a sixty-degree blind spot to his rear. Both eyes can be brought into play only on objects directly in front of the fish. For this reason the greatest areas of vision are seen with only one eye at a time. Through a study of his physical limitations, one can readily see that the trout is best approached from the rear. The extent of his view of things outside the stream is directly proportional to his depth in the water.

Sunshine and shadow greatly affect the vision of trout. They can be more easily taken when they are lying in bright sunlight than when they are in the shade. The reasons are rather obvious. Anything lying between the eye and the sun becomes blurred because of the glare. Conversely, the trout can see more clearly when there is less glare to confuse his eyesight.

Moving shadows are always a cause for alarm in the trout world. Shadows cast by anglers and natural enemies are equally alarming to the fish. Like other wild creatures, the trout is more alarmed by things that move rapidly. The deer-hunter knows this well. Floating leaders can cause large, alarming shadows too, while the sunken leader casts a thin shadow that may pass unnoticed by the most wary trout. The fear of shadows is easily understandable. The natural enemies of the trout have honed his reflexes to a fine edge.

Darkness is another factor affecting the wariness and vision of the trout. The large browns that warily hide under logs and boulders during the day will often forage boldly at night in water scarcely deep enough to keep them wet. The structure of the trout's eye makes it possible for him to see quite well at night. It is so fashioned that light is amplified, a peculiarity common among lesser animals.

Vision is not the only detection device available to the trout for survival. He is not physically equipped to hear sounds transmitted through the air, but he is easily alarmed by vibrations in the water. He perceives these with the sensitive lateral line that lies along his sides. Such things as clumsy wading, heavy feet on marshy banks, and the slash of a sloppy cast will send him scurrying for the nearest cover.

It is not intelligence as such that has made the trout such a cautious fish. The rigors of his existence have merely sharpened his instincts of self-preservation. The natural mortality of trout is extremely high. Dr. Paul R. Needham has gathered some amazing statistics on this subject. The average healthy female trout will lay from 500 to 1000 eggs for each pound of her weight. A rather small percentage of these eggs lives to hatch in the wild state. Eighty-five per cent of the fry that do hatch perish in the first eighteen months. Sixty per cent of all trout are winter-killed each year.

Those that live must survive collapsing snow banks, ice jams, anchor ice, freezing streams and other hazards of the winter. In the spring, they contend with torrential waters that grind up the stream bed and roll heavy boulders about with ease. During the summer months, they must cope with low water and warm temperatures.

These same grinding floods and droughts are extremely hard on the aquatic insects, too. These nymphs and larvae are scoured out of the stream bed in the spring and parboiled on the shallows in the summer. Rivers like the Schoharie suffer badly from these seasonal extremes. The last few years have been an excellent example. Not too many seasons ago the spring runoff scoured the bottom, and the hatches were very scattered. About the time that the stream had begun to come back, a drought reduced it to a mere trickle in July, with temperatures above eighty degrees. I talked with Art Flick that summer at Westkill, and he advised me not to waste my time on the stream.

"I love her so much I can't go look at her," he said. "The last brown I took didn't fight and wasn't worth eating. There won't be many hatches next year."

These seasonal problems are not the only factor affecting the food supply of the trout. The coarse fish compete with him for food, too. On a California research stream, one average-sized pool supported 684 fish. Only 46 were trout. Coarse fish are a problem on many streams, and we may be forced to find some means of reducing and controlling their numbers.

The visible rise of the trout to some form of insect life can be used to his disadvantage. There are several basic rise types that can be used by observant anglers to determine what the trout is doing. A man familiar with these rise types can save much time astream that would otherwise be wasted in experimentation. We all know that a rise is a visible disturbance of the surface made by a feeding trout.

Have you ever tried to pick up an insect from the surface of a stream? It is extremely difficult unless you catch it by the wings. Trying to let the insect float down into your palm sounds easy, but your hand splits the current and diverts the prey to one side. The trout is faced with the same problem. Nature has made it easy for him to catch the floating insect. He simply opens his gills and lets the water flow through, while the hapless insect floats right down his throat. Of course he may also pick a fly off the surface with precision, but this is most common in fast water, where he must hit or go hungry.

There are several elements affecting the character of a rise: the size of the natural, its action or lack of action, and its position with respect to the surface film. Large insects tend to provoke large, showy rises. Insects that flutter across the surface cause the trout to rise quickly to prevent their escape. Insects poised on the surface film, lying in the surface film, and drifting along beneath the surface film, all cause specific rise types. Of course the flying insect that flits across the surface, or rises and falls in the mating flight, causes the leap that carries an eager trout full length from the water.

Much speculation has been indulged in by anglers as to the motivation for the rise. As many as ten different drives found in the human have been ascribed to the trout, and it does not seem illogical to attribute rises to hunger and curiosity. Such discussions can never reach any concrete conclusions, but they lead to interesting hypotheses.

The important fact is that the trout do rise; why they rise is insignificant compared to this fortunate truth. We know that trout take the fly when they are actively feeding, and there is little doubt that this is due to hunger. And they will sometimes rise when they are not actively feeding. We can never know if this is caused by hunger or curiosity. Perhaps they would have been rising if a hatch had been present.

The suction rise is a type common to larger trout in more quiet water. There is an audible sucking sound that often leaves one or more bubbles behind it. This rise is usually to an insect resting in or on the surface film. The bubbles tell us which it was. In the suction rise, the bubbles are expelled through the gills of the trout, and are caused by the release of the air taken with the insect. If there are bubbles in the wake of the suction rise, it is not unlikely that the insect taken was riding on the surface film.

The smutting or dimple rise is common to quiet flats and pools. It consists of a tiny, quiet ring in the water, and is usually to a very small insect or a spent insect of some species. Dimple rises are calm and unhurried, and they often hide very large fish.

The dimpling swirl is often mistaken for a dimple rise, but it is caused by the trout taking some small insect form a few inches under the surface. It disturbs the water slightly a few moments after the actual rise, for there is a time lapse between the turning of the fish and the appearance of the swirl.

The common swirl rise is rather showy, and is often audible because of the enthusiasm with which it is executed. The swirl is caused by the taking of an insect near the surface and the return to the former position in the current. The swirl rise can be to nymphs or mature insects, and is usually to an active insect form rather than one that is drifting motionless. Again, the bubbles tell us whether the prey was a newly-hatched dun or a wriggling nymph.

The bulge rise is to food just under the surface, but it is completely unlike the common swirl rise. Where the common swirl is caused by the turning of the fish sideways under the surface, the bulge rise is caused by his arching back. Trout do not often break water with their heads, but dorsal fins and tails sometimes show above the surface. Fish rising in this manner appear to be lazily rolling over some underwater hurdle as a hunting horse takes a jump.

The head-and-tail rise is a surface rise that is quite similar to the bulge. It is common with large fish, and consists of the head, back and tail breaking water in quick succession. The performance is completed by what Ray Bergman aptly calls the "satisfaction rise" in his fine book, *Trout*. This is a little satisfied wiggle of the tail as the fish drops back into his feeding lie in the current. It is not a common rise except on the big pools in the West, where there are still large fish in fairly good numbers.

The slash rise occurs to fluttering or running insects. It also occurs in windy weather, when the fish are forced to strike quickly at insects that are being blown across the surface. One may often see the slash rise in fast water when a hatch of particularly large insects is present to excite the hunger of the trout.

The jump rise is to flying insects, those that have just hatched from the water, or those that have just touched the surface to deposit their eggs. Trout working in this manner are hard to catch, for it is difficult to simulate flight with an artificial fly. On the famous Lauterach, in southern Germany, there is a hatch and mating flight of large May flies each season. They emerge or mate in clouds of naturals, and the season when they are present over the water is called the *Sprungzeit*.

In the German, this means the "leaping time." The best way I found to take these leaping browns was to drop the fly quickly over a rise after the fish had taken a natural. The trout usually leaped again for the settling dry fly or met it as it touched the water. This sly technique was passed on by the old river-keeper who fished with me on the stream, and I have used it since with much success on American waters.

The tailing rise occurs only in shallow water, and is caused by trout nosing about in the bottom for nymphs and larvae. At such times, the tails break water and make a visible disturbance. Trout often dislodge food by tailing and then drop downstream quickly to feed on their results. At this instant an artificial nymph can be added to the drifting naturals. Tailing trout are not easily taken with a dry fly, but at times a juicy spider or variant will divert their attention.

The investigation rise is the first of a group of refusal rises that we shall consider. It is typical of large trout in smooth water. The fish rises to the fly and hangs cautiously below it in the current. If you have never experienced this with a large fish, you have no idea how unsettling it can be. Two things may happen after a refusal: the fish may return to his original position, or he may start back to his position and then turn with a sudden change of heart to take the fly hard.

The flash rise occurs below a floating fly or behind a sunken artificial that is being retrieved. It indicates interest in the fly. There is no disturbance of the surface, but one can see the flash of light as the trout turns. One should rest such a fish and try again with a smaller fly of the same pattern. The flash rise to spiders and variants is common, and has earned these flies the name of fish-finders. One can often locate large trout in this manner.

The splash rise to spiders and variants is also common, and it is often mistaken for a serious rise by many anglers. It consists of a splashy, half-hearted hit, and results in a missed fish. Even the average angler does not often miss trout if they really want the fly The splash rise is indicative of greater interest than the flash rise. It often means that the fly is rather close to what it should be in color, size and configuration. Nymphing trout will often respond to dry flies in this manner, and a nymph is well worth trying on a fish that rises in this way.

There is another rise that lies between the flash and the splash in character. It is the false rise, or *fausse montée,* as G. E. M. Skues has named it. It consists of a rise toward the fly, and then a rapid, alarmed retreat back to the feeding lie. This frightened turn often causes a swirl to appear on the surface; it can be mistaken for a rise if the light is such that only the surface is seen. If the fish is a good one, it will pay to rest him.

All of these different actions of feeding trout can be used to determine what fly and method should be used on a particular fish. The study of rise types is invaluable to the fisherman who often finds himself casting to specific fish. The great number of large, freely rising trout in the European chalk streams makes it rather easy to study rise types carefully there, and I was fortunate in spending two seasons fishing them. They taught me more about large, selective fish than any others of the many rivers I had fished.

Selectivity has long been one of the principal obstacles to continued fishing success. It consists of persistent refusal of all flies except those suggesting the particular insect form on which the fish is feeding. It is one reason why trout are not yet extinct. Faced with selectivity, the fisherman must determine two things: what the trout is taking, and what artificial he will accept in place of the natural.

It is true that there are times when the fish seem to take anything, but they are increasingly rare on most of our hard-pressed streams. Since selectivity is the big problem, it seems logical to prepare for it. The easy fishing that comes at other times is little challenge.

Selectivity has been attributed to many faculties of the trout. Some angling writers have speculated on its psychology, believing that a fish becomes accustomed to seeing a particular form above it on the surface, tries one or two, and then falls into a pattern that stimulates his feeding reflex only when that particular insect passes his position. On one occasion, on the Ausable in New York, my good friend Jeff Norton took a nice brown that was literally stuffed with caterpillars. The fish was feeding under the trees and contained nothing but these worms. None of the other trout caught by the party had indulged in these juicy morsels, although they were everywhere. It seems that the psychological feeding pattern may be an explanation of this one fish's behavior.

We have all seen days when the fish were rising to a certain insect not present in large numbers, paying no attention to other species that were on the water by the hundreds. This is rather difficult to explain. Trout often rise to tiny insects only, ignoring large, juicy naturals time after time. It is rather doubtful that we can ever understand these things, and I wonder if the answers would not dull our sport. Uncertainty and anticipation are a great part of our enjoyment.

Selective feeding gave birth to the theory of imitation. The exponents of this theory believe that a choosy fish can be taken only by exact simulation of his food. We know that trout can become extremely selective. We know that they can see color well. We also know that the fish can see colors at one end of the spectrum far better than we. Still, the most casual eye can see that our carefully tied imitations are far from being exact replicas of the naturals. This point is often stressed by opponents of the imitation theory. But do our flies have to be exact replicas? The idea of exact imitation is preposterous.

We know that trout are selective to specific hatches each year, and that during these times they can be taken only on certain flies. This cannot be explained without giving some credence to the imitationists. The word "imitation" seems to be the crux of our differences. The opponents of imitation argue that so-called imitations do not duplicate the natural prototypes. It is hardly important that the artificials do not look like naturals to them, for the trout is the final judge in such matters.

It appears, then, that the imitation theory needs some new phrasing. Flies that take selectively feeding trout seem to be *practical* imitations, and the fact that they are not *exact* imitations is unimportant. John Atherton, in his excellent book *The Fly and the Fish*, expresses the idea that the imitation theory is more nearly a theory of *impressionism*. He believes that flies tied to suggest the naturals are truly imitations in the practical sense of the word. They give the fish an impression of his food, and he is duped into rising. This seems to be the theory of imitation as it is practiced.

Selectivity and imitation are the biggest factors in trout fishing on our hard-fished waters. They are the dual reasons for this book, for the study of insect life would be pointless if they did not exist. Stream entomology would be of little interest to the angler, as would the hundreds of fly patterns created over the years.

Fortunately, the sport is not that simple. Trout are wary and selective, particularly on water that has heavy fishing pressure. They are so wary that anglers have trouble fooling

---

PLATE ONE: MAY FLIES *(opposite)*

Epeorus pleuralis male dun; *Epeorus pleuralis* female dun; *Paraleptophlebia adoptiva* male dun; *Paraleptophlebia adoptiva* female dun; *Epeorus vitrea* male dun.

Epeorus vitrea female dun; *Iron fraudator* male dun; *Iron fraudator* female dun; *Ephemerella subvaria* male dun; *Ephemerella subvaria* female dun.

Leptophlebia cupida male dun; *Leptophlebia cupida* female dun; *Stenonema vicarium* male dun; *Stenonema vicarium* female dun; *Ephemerella dorothea* male dun.

Stenonema fuscum male dun; *Stenonema fuscum* female dun; *Paraleptophlebia mollis* male dun; *Paraleptophlebia mollis* female dun; *Ephemerella dorothea* female dun.

Ephemera guttulata male dun; *Ephemera guttulata* female dun; *Ephemerella attenuata* female dun; *Ephemerella attenuata* male dun; *Leptophlebia johnsoni* male dun.

Isonychia bicolor male dun; *Isonychia bicolor* female dun; *Hexagenia recurvata* male dun; *Hexagenia recurvata* female dun; *Leptophlebia johnsoni* female dun.

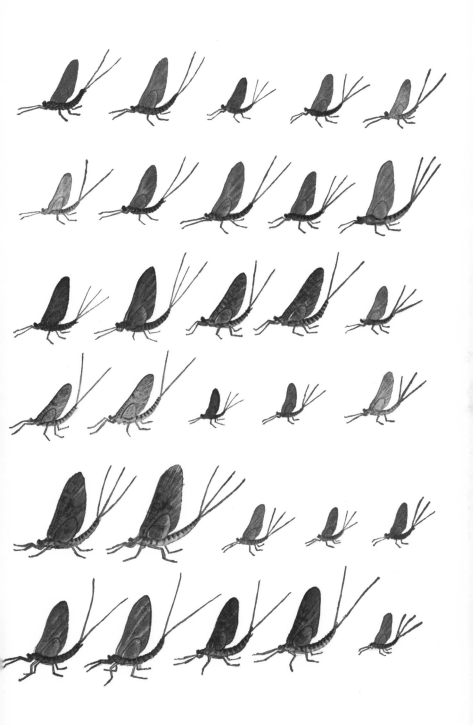

them consistently. Figures compiled in Michigan along an experimental stream show that half of the fishermen caught no legal fish. The 2 per cent considered expert by the research specialists accounted for 17 per cent of the total season's catch. These figures indicate that trout-fishing luck consists of finding the fish in a feeding mood. Skill and knowledge are responsible for further success.

Before one can become proficient at anything, he must want to put forth the effort required. One can never learn all there is to know about trout, but each bit of knowledge absorbed can be applied later with deadly effect. When you start to analyze your fishing as you would the slice in your golf game, you are on the right track. Armchair fishing can be almost as much fun as the real thing, and it can increase your efficiency.

We have seen in this chapter that the trout is shy and sophisticated. To overcome his sophistication, we must study his habits carefully. His biggest advantage is selectivity, and we can counteract it only by knowing the insects that make up his diet. This is the reason for the study of stream entomology by the angler, and it is often the weak link in his skill. All of his other skills are aimed at getting the fly over a fish that is not yet aware of his presence. They are of little value if that carefully presented fly is not one that the trout wants. Stream tactics can be learned by experience, but stream entomology can be learned only by serious study.

The idea that trout are difficult to catch is not a very new one. Charles Cotton emphasized fine tackle and imitation in 1676. His approach was born of respect for a noble and wary fish. The trout may have a brain that is only the size of a large pea, but he has made some confident and intelligent specimens of *Homo sapiens* look rather foolish in the past.

THE PRINCIPAL STREAM INSECTS

THE TROUT FISHERMAN is primarily concerned with the three common aquatic orders of stream insects: the stone flies, caddis flies and May flies. Of these three orders, the May flies are by far the most important.

It is true that trout feed regularly upon the other aquatic and some nonaquatic orders. In many years of fishing I have recorded only eight instances of heavy feeding on insects of the lesser aquatic species and land species. It seems obvious that our principal interest is in stone flies, caddis flies and May flies. These three insect orders have been grouped in this chapter to prepare the reader for detailed discussion later in the book.

The importance of aquatic insects in the trout diet becomes apparent when we consider the high milligram-for-milligram food value of these hexapods, compared to other staple items in their food. The insect population on our better streams is sufficient to sustain even the largest fish. Research has shown that the immature stages of stream insects are so numerous that each acre of bottom conceals about 100 pounds of nymphs and larvae. Particularly rich streams may have as much as 200 pounds per acre of bottom.

The aquatic insects spend all but a few days of their lives under water. For this reason trout do most of their feeding beneath the surface. The logical conclusion that may be reached from this fact may be rather disillusioning to the dry-fly purist. His favorite lure is suggestive of adult insect stages, which are available to feeding trout for a relatively brief period of time. The immature stages of these same insects are to be had by hungry fish during the rest of the entire year. The dry-fly purist is placing his chances for success on the short end of some rather impressive odds. He is benefiting from only 10 to 25 per cent of feeding activity.

Since the devotee of the wet fly uses patterns suggestive of drowned adults, clumsy land insects, species that emerge under water, or those species that lay their eggs under water, he is also restricting his sport. Drowned adult insects are not too common, land insects do not make up a major part of the trout diet, not many species emerge under water, and few species go under water to lay their eggs. Some wet-fly patterns are suggestive of nymph life, and are really nymphs in the true sense of the word. Wet-fly fishermen who point to success with these patterns are in actuality nymph fishermen.

The angler talented in fishing nymph and larva imitations is the man who will take trout consistently throughout the season. He can accomplish this because he is fishing patterns suggestive of the bulk of the trout diet. Any angler versed in nymph fishing is aware of this, and it is rare indeed that trout do not respond to this deadliest of trouting techniques.

Although fishing the dry fly is admittedly the most charming method, it is not the most difficult method of fly-fishing for trout. Its great attraction lies in the fact that the rise is on the surface, and all anglers will agree that this is thrilling. Yet the only challenge in dry-fly fishing is the dragless float. The upstream dead-drift nymph is far more difficult to fish.

Getting back to the natural insects, the stone flies, caddis flies and May flies are insects whose immature stages are wholly aquatic. The immature stages of stone flies and May flies are called "nymphs." They are found principally in the faster water, although some species are exceptions to this rule of thumb. The immature stages of the caddis flies are called "worms" by the fisherman and "larvae" by the entomologist.

The aquatic insects are distinctly a minority when compared with their terrestrial cousins. They are not found in extremely deep water or far from shore. The adult stages leave the water to reproduce and perish. In this stage they breathe air and do little feeding. No feeding is done by the May flies after the final moulting, for the mouth becomes atrophied and useless.

Some aquatic insect orders have complete metamorphosis, others incomplete. There are four stages in the complete life cycle: egg, larva, pupa and adult. The incomplete cycle consists of egg, nymph and adult. Both the stone flies and May flies have incomplete life cycles, while the caddis flies have complete life cycles.

In these three orders the anatomy is essentially the same. On the head are the "feelers" or antennae, simple eyes and compound eyes. The mouth parts are rather complex and unimportant to the angler. The *thorax* bears the six legs and consists of three segments: *protothorax, mesothorax* and *metathorax.* The thorax also bears the wings. The abdomen consists of many segments. The back parts are called *tergites,* the belly segments are called *sternites* and the side parts are the *pleurae.* At the rear of the abdomen are the tails. The legs are complex and rather unimportant to the fisherman. He should know that the upper leg is the *femur* and the lower leg is the *tibia,* for purposes of description.

Developing wings or wing cases are found on the thorax of the stone fly and May fly nymph. They are rather prominent on the immature insects and become quite dark just before the time of emergence. When the emergence occurs these wing cases split open, and the adult insect wriggles out of its nymphal skin.

The wings of insects are composed of integument, veins and nervures. The vein pattern is often important in the identification of the species, and it will be discussed later in this book.

Nymphs and larvae breathe under water through gills that are located variously, depending upon the species. Most May flies have gills along the abdomen; stone flies have hairy gills under the thorax (though a few species lack these appendages); and caddis flies have hairy gills along the entire body. These gills are so delicate that oxygen is absorbed into them.

The eggs of aquatic insects are quite amazing. Within individual species one finds ingenious safety devices that rival some of man's best contrivances. Those of some species have little vinelike threads that attach themselves to water plants, and others have little floats that buoy them up in the water.

After the nymphs or larvae have hatched from the eggs, they go through many moultings in their steady growth to adult size. After each moulting the immature form grows to the elastic limit of its skin and moults again. The final shedding of the skin reveals the winged adult in the stone flies and caddis flies. The winged May flies go through one more moulting after emergence.

General characteristics of the important aquatic insects have been treated thus far. Specific habits of the three orders will be discussed in the pages that follow, and individual habits will be covered in later chapters.

Plecoptera (Stone Flies)

Immature Plecoptera are known as nymphs. They are found in the swifter portions of the stream: the riffles, runs

Stone Fly Nymph

and pocket water. These nymphs cling to the stones and logs in these stretches. When fully grown they vary from less than a half inch to two inches in length, according to species.

Nymphs may be recognized by their prominent tails and
feelers and the twin sets of wing cases. Closer study will dis-
close in most species the hairy gills concentrated under the
thorax. Two claws on each foot are another characteristic of
the stone flies.

In general coloration many of the species are similar, with
ornamental marking about the wing cases and a distinct ringing of the body. They are generally amber to brown in hue,
with a slight paling on the undersides. A few species show almost uniform color—cream, amber, blackish brown.

Emergence of the Plecoptera occurs sporadically throughout
the season. When the emergence time is near, the nymph
crawls from his hiding place on the bottom and migrates to
the shallows. There he climbs out of the water and secretes a
gluelike substance, which anchors his nymphal skin to a
chosen rock. The thorax then splits and the adult stone fly
crawls out, leaving the shuck behind him. These empty shucks
are often quite lifelike in appearance, and for some unknown
reason they seem to be concentrated on certain rocks. All
anglers are familar with these empty skins, and have often
been puzzled by the popularity of special emergence spots.

Stone flies seem to emerge in good numbers during the
early morning hours. Artificials are often quite effective at
these times. Since great numbers of the nymphs are dislodged
and injured in high water, the imitations are excellent after
freshets. Weighted imitations are deadly early in the season;
they should be fished in the deep water
below swift riffles and runs. Little or no
motion should be imparted to the imitation. Contrary to much that has been
written about nymphing, the strikes are
often rather vicious in such fishing.

Adult Stone Fly in Flight

Adult stone flies are rather clumsy fliers
and swift, elusive runners. They have two
pairs of wings that are quite prominent in flight, and fly slowly
with their bodies in an almost vertical position. The wings are

heavy and coarse compared to those of the spritely May flies. When resting or riding the current, stone flies fold their wings flat over their bodies, giving the appearance of having only one pair.

The stone flies do not rank with the May flies and caddis flies as trout food, but on streams where they are numerous they are important. Notable examples of this are seen during the mating flights on Western rivers. These flights are known as salmon fly or willow fly hatches. Nymphs of the stone fly are often incorrectly called hellgrammites by trout fishermen, particularly on Western streams.

Stone flies cannot be raised in captivity without fast water, and aquarium study of them is difficult. Screen cages anchored in the stream are the easiest means of keeping live stone fly nymphs. When placed in still water, they writhe violently to create circulation over their filament-like gills.

The nymphs are distrustful of light, and scurry back to the dark side of rocks overturned in collecting work. They are for the most part vegetarians, but some of the larger species have carnivorous and even cannibalistic tendencies. Adult stone flies move about very little, preferring to rest along the stream. They are rarely over the water in great numbers except during the mating flights. Their chief value as trout food occurs during this time.

Caddis Larvae and Their Cases

Trichoptera (Caddis Flies)

The larvae of the caddis fly order are an intriguing clan. Almost every genus builds its own characteristic larval case from gravel, sand or plant residue. On streams or lakes having brightly colored gravel, these little cases are quite striking. Caddis fly larvae are known to fishermen as water worms, caddis worms, caddis creepers and periwinkles. They vary from about one-quarter inch to two inches in length. The little protective cases are cemented together with glandular secretions. The outsides are often very rough in appearance, but the insides are quite smooth and allow the larvae freedom of movement. Some species do not build cases at all, but hide among the debris of the bottom.

The caddis fly larvae are generally pale worms with hooks at the rear of their bodies, which anchor them within their cases. The larvae have dark heads and six legs attached to a dark thorax. The gills are hairy and distributed along the abdomen.

When the larvae grow too large for their cases, they add to them or discard them for new ones. The worms do not fit tightly into the cases, so the current may pass through. They usually lie with head, thorax and legs outside their cases. The body is gently undulated to keep the water circulating through the gills. Larvae will retreat turtle-like into their cases if disturbed, and can be removed only by dismantling the cases themselves.

Since the Trichoptera have a complete life cycle, there is also a pupal stage of growth. The pupal period lasts about two weeks, and there is quite a transformation during that time. The adult configuration begins to appear inside the pupal skin. During pupation the larvae are sealed tightly from everything but a trickle of water. When the period is complete, the heavy-jawed larvae have been transformed into mothlike adults. Swift-water species swim to the surface and emerge from the pupal skin. Slow-water species crawl to the shallows and emerge much like stone flies. The emergence of the caddis flies is an important time to anglers, for the pupae are migrating to the surface *en masse*.

Adult caddis flies are often called "sedges" by trout fishermen, and they are over the water in clouds when the egg-laying occurs. The wings are folded tentlike over the abdomen when the insects are on the water or resting in the streamside brush. Caddis flies are second only to the May flies as trout food. They are often present in unbelievable numbers in the evening, heading into the wind in clouds, as on the famous Frying Pan in Colorado on July evenings.

Some species oviposit over the water and others dip the eggs into the stream itself. Certain species go under water to lay their eggs, and do not return to the air after they have finished. Imitations of caddis fly adults are effective in both dry- and wet-fly versions, both types tied downwing style.

Some species emerge at a given time each

Adult Caddis Fly at Rest

year, forming the familiar hatches known to the fisherman. Others are found sporadically over the water during the season, and are not as important as trout food.

Ephemeroptera (May Flies)

The May flies are the most important aquatic insects from the fisherman's viewpoint. They are the prototypes for many of our popular fly patterns. Trout are often highly selective to May flies, and feed upon them to the exclusion of other orders.

A striking example of this May fly preference occurs on the Colorado Frying Pan. On the famous Pan, as it is known affectionately by my Western fishing friends, there are heavy flights of caddis flies each evening in July. The fish rise well to these caddises during the late afternoon and early evening, but they pay little attention to them after the first May flies begin to emerge. These May fly hatches are not heavy, being only about 20 per cent of the fly life present, but the trout rise to them with great selectivity.

Experiments conducted by our party in 1948 showed that flies tied to imitate the caddis flies worked well until the May flies appeared. After that, the trout could be taken only on flies tied to imitate the May flies present. I have seen trout excercise this feeding whim often on widely separated streams, and it is reasonable to state the trout preference for the May flies as an angling hypothesis.

Like the other orders we have discussed, the May flies spend most of their lives under water. In the immature stages, they are called nymphs. The nymphs are very shy and hide carefully on the bottom until it is time for them to emerge. As this period draws near they lose their timidity and become quite active in the water. At these times an artificial nymph is excellent.

May flies have an incomplete life cycle of egg, nymph and adult. The eggs are deposited in the water by the females and hatch into young nymphs. These have several markedly different shapes, depending upon the family. May flies have been classified into several families, which have quite different nymphal habits. Those with burrowing nymphs are the *Ephemeridae;* those with clinging nymphs are known as *Heptagenidae;* and those with crawling, swimming nymphs have been designated *Baetidae.*

May flies consume diatoms and desmids in large quantities for food, and their diet is largely vegetarian. Growth is rapid, with the nymph outgrowing and shedding his nymphal skin as often as twenty times.

The May fly nymphs have bodies of ten segments, with their gills distributed variously according to the different genera. The thorax is very muscular and supports the growing wings under the dark wing cases. Most nymphs have three tails, but some species have only two.

As we have seen before, the nymphs become quite restless prior to ecdysis. Slow-water species, which are easily kept alive for aquarium study, often make several trips to the surface before actually emerging. Trout have a great opportunity for nymph feeding when such occurences take place in the water. The gently retrieved May fly nymph is a deadly artificial at these times.

When the nymph reaches the surface to emerge, he splits his nymphal shuck at the thorax, and the surface tension literally peels him out of the old skin. The freshly hatched May fly then pops out on the surface; and as soon as his wings are sufficiently dried, he takes to the air. The drying period is not long, often lasting only a few seconds.

This stage of the May fly is known as *dun* by the trout fisherman, and its scientific name is *subimago*. Duns may be recognized by their generally dull coloring and underdeveloped wing venation. Most species make a direct flight to the shoreline brush to rest before the final moulting, but a few species moult immediately and mate. If the duns escape the trout and birds to reach the comparative safety of the streamside bushes, they rest before the final moult and mating flights. The final moulting takes place from twenty minutes to three days later, depending upon species. After this is completed the dun reappears as a *spinner* or *imago* May fly. Since the spinners come out of the brush for the mating flight, fishermen often refer to them as a "brush hatch." Trout do not often feed upon spinners until after the mating, when they lie spent on the water. As my friend Art Flick points out in the *Streamside Guide*, the imago flies are in the air and not on the water, and this is the reason the fish do not rise to them often.

Some species dip their eggs into the water after the mating flight, or ride the current while ovipositing. Such species are readily available to the fish, and are of greater importance than the others.

To digress for a moment, it might be worth while to describe some of the signs that appear in nature before a hatch of flies. Nymphs that are about to emerge have very dark wing cases, and if one knows what the adult insect is like he can prepare himself. All observant fishermen have seen the restlessness of the birds just before hatches begin. They hop nervously from twig to rock and back again, and dart across the surface of the water. Somehow they seem to feel the emergence time approaching. When the flies start to appear, the birds wheel back and forth over the water competing with the fish for the emerging duns. One should always watch the birds along the water.

Many spinners are often so different from their dun stage that fishermen do not believe they are the same species. The tails become long and dainty, the abdomens long and delicate; the coloring is quite different in many cases, and the forelegs of the males become quite long.

The anatomy of the adult May fly is exquisite. On the water he looks like a delicate little sailboat. May flies have four wings, like the caddis flies and stone flies, but in the May fly the rear wings are quite small. Several very small genera have only two wings, but they are for the most part of little interest to the angler.

Mating May Flies

May flies mate in the afternoon and early evening during most of the season. The nuptial dance is quite striking. Mating takes place over the stream, with the males rising and falling in a swarm above the water. Females fly into the swarm to secure mates. The male spinner grasps the female by her thorax with his long forelegs and bends his body back until contact with the egg mass is made by the caliper-like forceps at the extremity of his abdomen. Once joined, they leave the swarm, with the larger female supporting both insects in flight. After the fertilization is completed the male flies off in search of another mate, and the female deposits her eggs into the water.

The eggs are extruded through an opening on the underside of the female, between the seventh and eighth abdominal segments. Some species extrude the eggs into little egg sacs before dropping them into the water.

Spinners of one genus actually go under the water to lay their eggs. They rarely return to the surface, but drift along drowned in the current. Most spinners lie spent on the water after the nuptial flight, but some of the males may be present for several days.

May flies require fresh, clean water in which to live, and in most such waters they far outnumber other insect orders. If it were not for the great numbers devoured by the fish, birds and carnivorous insects, they would be present in fantastic multitudes.

The angler fortunate enough to find a heavy hatch in progress will have some rare sport if he has the proper May fly imitation and the skill to present his fly cleverly to the trout.

EASTERN MAY FLIES: EARLY SEASON

ON THOSE BRIGHT, blustery days of early season, the first of the May flies start to emerge. Early hatches are often surprisingly heavy regardless of the weather, and the angler who has ventured out is often rewarded with some excellent fishing.

There is never much May fly activity until the water has warmed to the fifty-degree mark, and the heaviest early-spring hatches emerge at midday.

The unreliable weather of late April and early May can produce real problems for the angler, but only high, dirty water is a serious obstacle to success. Cold, wet days retard the drying of the wings, and the freshly emerged duns are forced to remain on the water longer. This often tempts fish to surface-feed long before the water has reached what are commonly considered dry-fly conditions.

Many things other than the actual fishing are a cause for pleasure in early season. Many things can add to acute discomfort as well. One can be faced with balmy weather at midday and near-Arctic conditions by late afternoon. But to the angler, being present along the stream in that indefinable awakening of spring is refreshing in itself. The perceptive soul can feel new life in the stirring out-of-doors, and can feel the approaching summer in those indescribable winds from the south. Even when the trout are not cooperating well, the angler can find pleasure in a hint of new green in the branches above the water, or in a cluster of early violets in a sheltered spot. And the bright spring sunshine is an added bonus to the man who is tired of the bleak, grimy days of city winter.

Epeorus pleuralis (Family Heptagenidae)

This medium-sized May fly is the first insect of major importance on Eastern trout streams, and it is often present when banks of snow still lie in places sheltered from the midday sun. The hatches usually occur during the last week in April, but specimens are sometimes found emerging well into May.

The delicate little duns are known by many names on various streams, but the most common one is the Gordon Quill. Other local names are Blue Quill, Grey Quill and Blue Dun.

These May flies are very susceptible to temperature change and require fast, pure water. They die quickly in still or slightly polluted water, and are very difficult to raise in captivity for these reasons. Streams having good hatches are the Beaverkill, Willowemoc, Esopus, Schoharie and Brodhead in New York and Pennsylvania.

Unlike many May flies, *Epeorus pleuralis* emerges at almost the same time each day. There is an occasional hatch late in the morning, but the trout are rarely disposed to rise during that activity. The main emergence comes between one and two in the afternoon. Anglers can look for these May flies at any time after the streams have passed the fifty-degree mark. About two or three days of such stream temperatures and one can expect good hatching activity.

An unusual habit of the genus is emergence under water. The nymphs crawl to the downstream side of underwater rocks to split the nymphal skins. Then the duns struggle to the surface, making a wet fly suggestive of them an extremely killing pattern. The nymph imitation is of little value during emergence.

Nymph imitations are most effective later in the season, when large numbers of nymphs are present from the preceding egg-laying. These are small patterns suggestive of partly grown nymphs, and they are very effective during the low-water months.

The nymphs are of the broad, flat type with prominent gills that help to form a suction on the face of the rocks. They are greyish tan, with darker rings between the body segments. The legs are greyish tan with brown mottling on the femora, which are flat and heavy in appearance. The thorax is broad with dark brownish wing cases. The eyes are large and dark, and the two tails are flecked like wood-duck flank fibers.

Epeorus Nymph

My favorite sizes in the artificial are 14 and 16, fished dead-drift in the riffles and runs. The rise to the dead-drift nymph in low water is very quiet, and must be sensed rather than seen in many cases. The flash of the fish in the current, or the twitch and pause of the float, are the subtle clues. It takes patience and practice to bring your senses to the fine edge required.

Although the Epeorus Nymph is not too useful during emergence, a wet fly suggestive of the duns emerging under water is often deadly. Many of these duns never reach the air, but drift helplessly along under water. The duns are quite bedraggled before they reach the surface to dry their wings, and a well-chewed version of the famous Hare's Ear is my favorite imitation. It should be dressed on size 12 and 14 hooks. Since these duns are often struggling under water, an occasional twitch is needed.

Since taking early-season trout on the dry fly is undeniably more fun than fishing wet, the duns of this hatch are well loved. They ride the current for some time before flying off, and entice the fish to rise even in the most inclement weather.

Male Subimago or Dun

Tails—three-eighths inch, brownish grey
Body—five-sixteenths inch, greyish yellow with dark brownish rings at the segments
Legs—greyish tan with brown mottlings
Thorax—dark greyish bronze
Eyes—large and dark
Wings—dark greyish blue, three-eighths inch

Female Subimago or Dun

Tails—seven-sixteenths inch, brownish grey
Body—three-eighths inch, greyish yellow with dark brownish rings at the segments
Legs—greyish tan with brown mottlings
Thorax—dark greyish bronze
Eyes—small and greyish
Wings—seven-sixteenths inch, greyish blue

My favorite imitation of the male dun is the Dark Gordon Quill in size 14. The female is slightly larger and paler, and my favorite pattern is the standard Gordon Quill tied in size 12.

Approximately two days after the duns have hatched, they reappear over the water as spinners. The fishermen on many streams now know them as Red Quill Spinners, and they are often important as early-season food. The mating flight occurs at midday.

Male Imago or Spinner

Tails—one-half inch, dark brownish
Body—five-sixteenths inch, greyish yellow with dark brownish red rings at the segments
Legs—greyish tan with brown mottling
Thorax—dark reddish brown
Eyes—large and blackish
Wings—glassy clear, three-eighths inch

Female Imago or Spinner

Tails—seven-sixteenths inch, dark brownish
Body—three-eighths inch, greyish yellow with brownish red
　ringing and a touch of tan at the rear
Legs—greyish tan with brown mottling
Thorax—dark reddish brown
Eyes—small and dark grey
Wings—glassy clear, seven-sixteenths inch

The Red Quill Spinner is an excellent imitation in sizes 12
and 14. Both dry- and wet-fly versions are of great value to
the fisherman. The Female Red Quill Spinner in size 12 is
a good female likeness.

Notes taken over a five-season period indicate that *Epeorus
pleuralis* emerges during the last week in April and the first
week in May. Scattered hatching is found earlier and later,
but the heaviest activity occurs during the two weeks at the
turn of the month.

Paraleptophlebia adoptiva (Family Baetidae)

This diminutive species is one of the earliest to appear on
Eastern trout waters. It is often found as early as the third

*Paralepto-
phlebia
Nymph*

week in April. Trout seem to be quite fond of these
little May flies, and I have seen them ignore larger
insects to feed upon them. They seem to be present
in all types of water, but the stretches of medium current speed have the heaviest concentrations. Emergence usually begins at eleven o'clock in the morning
and lasts for the rest of the day. The heaviest hatches
are at midday.

Anglers usually find these hatches rather perplexing, for imitations larger than size 16 are ignored by
the fish. Few are equipped with flies smaller than that, and
following their float on anything but still water is extremely
difficult.

The nymphs are of the creeping type, and drag their low-
slung bodies clumsily over the bottom. The thorax is a dirty

tannish grey, the abdomen is greyish with darker brownish
rings at the segments, the legs are tannish grey, the wing cases
are dark greyish brown, the gills are thick and greyish brown,
and the three tails are yellowish brown. These nymphs are well
imitated by the Leptophlebia Nymph in sizes 16 and 18. This
should be fished upstream dead-drift, and is particularly effective when fished through actual rises during the hatching
activity.

Male Subimago or Dun

Tails—one-quarter inch, light greyish
Body—five-sixteenths inch, greyish with distinct ringing at the
   abdominal segments
Legs—medium grey-brown
Thorax—greyish brown
Eyes—large and greyish brown
Wings—five-sixteenths inch, dark bluish grey

Female Subimago or Dun

Tails—one-quarter inch, light greyish
Body—five-sixteenths inch, greyish with distinct brownish
   ringing at the abdominal segments
Legs—medium greyish brown
Thorax—distinctly brownish
Eyes—small and greyish
Wings—three-eighths inch, dark bluish grey

Some local names for these little duns are Iron Blue Dun,
Blue Dun and Little Blue May fly. The males are imitated by
a Dark Blue Quill in size 20. The females are imitated by a
Dark Red Quill in size 18.

Four days after hatching out as duns, these flies return to
the stream in the spinner stage. Since they are over the water
for as much as a week, these little imago May flies are sometimes important.

Male Imago or Spinner

Tails—three-eighths inch, light greyish
Body—five-sixteenths inch, greyish with distinct dark greyish
   rings at the abdominal segments

Legs—medium greyish brown
Thorax—greyish brown
Eyes—large and dark greyish brown
Wings—five-sixteenths inch, glassy clear

Female Imago or Spinner
Tails—one-quarter inch, light greyish
Body—five-sixteenths inch, greyish with distinct brownish
    ringing at the abdominal segments
Legs—medium greyish grown
Thorax—greyish brown
Eyes—small and greyish
Wings—three-eighths inch, glassy clear

The Blue Quill Spinner is an excellent imitation of the male
imago in size 20. The Female Blue Quill Spinner is killing in
size 18. These spinners dip into the water to lay their eggs,
and if there are no other insects on the water, they become
important.

Paraleptophlebia adoptiva emerges on Eastern waters from the
third week in April until the middle of May. These averages
are based upon observations in three seasons of hatching.

Iron fraudator (Heptagenidae Family)

This slate-colored May fly is very closely related to *Epeorus
pleuralis,* and for practical angling purposes they are identical
flies. The principal differences are in the nymphal stages, and
are visible without magnification. Nymphs of the related genus
or subgenus *Iron* are longer, and do not appear to be as heavy.
The tips of the gills curve in sharply toward the abdomen.
There is a single mark on each femur.

Epeorus nymphs are mottled on each femur, the gills are
broad and flat, and the femora are thick and heavy in appearance. Distinguishing the adults is more difficult, but the markings on the femora are often distinct enough for differentiation
between species.

The general configuration of the *Iron* nymph has already
been discussed. The wing cases are dark greyish brown, the

bodies are greyish brown with dark ringing at the segments, the thorax is brownish grey, the legs are greyish tan with the single brown mark on each femur, the eyes are greyish, and there are two mottled tails. The Iron Nymph artificial is excellent in sizes 12 and 14.

Except for the differences already treated, the duns are quite like those of *Epeorus pleuralis* in coloring and habits. The Dark Gordon Quill in size 14 imitates the males, and the Gordon Quill in size 12 matches the female. In the imago stage, the Red Quill Spinner in size 12 is an excellent imitation of the females.

Iron Nymph

These spinners reappear over the stream about two days after they first emerge, and they mate over the riffles at midday. Trout often rise rather well to these early-season spinner flights.

The difference between the genus *Epeorus* and its relative *Iron* was unknown to me until very recently, and my notes concerning the latter are meager. Since I formerly included them in the same category, my notes are undoubtedly full of *Iron* hatches listed as *Epeorus*. Two seasons of data seem to indicate that they emerge in the third week in April, and are present until the third week in May. The heaviest hatches occur early in that month.

Ephemerella subvaria (Family Baetidae)

This hatch is found on most Eastern streams from the end of April until the fourth week in May. Notes also show it to have been present on Adirondack streams as late as the first week in June.

It is more important to the fly fisherman than any of the preceding species. It is more widely distributed, is larger in size, and emerges when most of the streams are reaching optimum conditions.

Ephemerella subvaria is found emerging with two related species, *Ephemerella invaria* and *Ephemerella rotunda; subvaria* is the most common of the three. They are being treated together, since telling these May flies apart is a task for the venation specialists.

The hatches are known to trout addicts as the Hendricksons, but one can always find an old-timer along some Catskill river who calls them Whirling Duns.

An interesting characteristic is the radically different coloring of males and females. The two sexes seem to emerge from different parts of the stream. This can mean that fish in one stretch of water will be selective to females only, while trout in the water above are feeding upon the male duns.

Both males and females emerge around two o'clock in the afternoon, and they remain on the water for about an hour of activity. Often they will be found emerging with stragglers from preceding May fly species.

The nymphs of these *Ephemerella* May flies are very active in the hour preceding emergence, and nymphal imitations

prove quite killing at these times. These nymphs are of the slow-water-dwelling *Baetidae,* and may be found in the silt and trash that lie among still-water rocks. They also emerge in lesser numbers from the eddies of the fast-water sections of the stream.

These nymphs are about three-eighths inch in length, and are not as flat in appearance as the earlier species. They emerge by wriggling to the surface, where they split the nymphal skins and appear as winged duns. Nymph artificials are effective, fished either dead-drift or with a very slight retrieve suggestive of the struggle to the surface.

Ephemerella Nymph, Invaria Group

The abdomens are a tannish cream with a ruddy cast, and the back segments are a ruddy brownish grey. The gills are brownish grey, and the three tails are a mottled tannish grey. The wing cases are a dark brownish grey and the thorax is a brownish grey. The gills and legs are not so prominent in this genus as in *Iron* and *Epeorus.*

The Dark Ephemerella Nymph in sizes 12 and 14 is effective both before and during a hatch. If the angler desires to work the deeper water where these nymphs are found in good numbers, the hooks may be weighted by winding the tying silk tightly around two pieces of fuse wire set in cement along the sides of the hook shank. This will also give the nymphs a flattened look. Unweighted versions are often deadly during actual emergence, for the trout often never bother with the duns, preferring to feed upon the nymphs that are rising from the bottom.

Male Subimago or Dun

Tails—tannish grey flecked with brown, seven-sixteenths inch
Body—five-sixteenths inch, light reddish brown distinctly ringed
Legs—dirty tannish grey
Thorax—ruddy brownish grey
Eyes—deep brownish and large
Wings—medium bluish grey, three-eighths inch

Female Subimago or Dun

Tails—three-eighths inch, tannish grey flecked with light brownish markings
Body—creamish grey with an elusive pinkish cast, three-eighths inch, darker brownish grey back markings
Legs—dirty tannish grey
Thorax—creamish grey with a ruddy tinge
Eyes—yellowish grey and small
Wings—medium bluish grey, one-half inch

The well-loved Red Quill dry fly created by Art Flick is my favorite imitation for the male duns. It was first dressed as an imitation of *Ephemerella subvaria*. I have one of the old master's flies before me as I write, and its stiff, sparse hackle and delicate dressing are well suited to the still waters and educated browns of the Schoharie. It is best in size 14. The female dun is well imitated by the reliable Hendrickson, first tied by Roy Steenrod on the Beaverkill in 1916. It was christened after Albert Everett Hendrickson, one of the anglers of the Theo-

dore Gordon era along the Catskill rivers. The Hendrickson
should be tied in sizes 12 and 14 to imitate these female duns.

These two dry-fly patterns should be alternated in fishing
as a change of pace. Since the males and females emerge from
different stretches and at different times, it is wise to try both
flies over a choosy brown before damning his eyesight and
moving on.

The imago stages of this hatch are not too important to the
angler, for the females drop their eggs from the air in clusters.
They are rarely on the water in any numbers until they are
spent after mating. The days of spring can be blustery, and
the wind sometimes blows the egg-laden spinners into the
water in good numbers, and the trout feed eagerly upon them
at such times.

Male Imago or Spinner

Tails—five-eighths inch, tannish grey flecked with brown
   mottlings
Body—five-sixteenths inch, ruddy brown with distinct ringing
   at the abdominal segments
Legs—greyish brown
Thorax—rusty brown
Eyes—large and dark brownish
Wings—clear and glassy, three-eighths inch.

Female Imago or Spinner

Tails—seven-sixteenths inch, tannish grey flecked with brown-
   ish mottlings
Body—three-eighths inch, yellowish cream with a pale yellow
   egg sac formed at the rear extremity
Legs—yellowish grey
Thorax—dirty yellowish grey
Eyes—small and greyish
Wings—one-half inch, clear and glassy

The Little Rusty Spinner is my favorite imitation of the
males in size 14. The Female Hendrickson is a killing representation of the females in sizes 12 and 14.

I had always regarded these heavy spinner flights as an

interesting but unimportant phenomenon until one windy day on the Ausable in New York. I had fished all day with little success, although the trout were rising well. Nymphs did little business with anything but small fish, and the only naturals I saw were mating spinners. Later in the afternoon, when no more rises were to be seen, I met an old man along one of the East Branch flats. He had six browns between twelve and fifteen inches. When I asked incredulously what they had taken, he showed me a well-chewed Lady Beaverkill wet fly that he had patiently fished among the rocks.

Stream notes indicate that these *Ephemerella* hatches occur from the end of April until the end of May. In five seasons there have been two exceptions: one early hatch in late April and one hatch in June. The wide distribution of these insects and their long period of emergence make them of great importance to the angler.

Leptophlebia cupida (Family Baetidae)

This fairly large May fly was formerly classified as *Blasturus cupidus,* but it has recently been assigned to the genus *Leptophlebia* by the entomologists. It is common on Eastern trout waters.

Two characteristics make the adult and nymph stages easily recognized: the adults have three tails with the center tail shorter than the others, and the nymphs have large, leaflike double gills. The nymphs are hardy little creatures and will live for weeks in unchanged water. They do not hide from their enemies, but range freely about, relying solely on protective coloration.

Leptophlebia Nymph

The nymphs are about five-eighths inch in length, and are generally dark chestnut brown in color. The body and gills are this deep ruddy color. The thorax and wing cases are almost black. The legs and tails are brown, and the eyes are blackish brown.

The Dark Leptophlebia Nymph is an excellent imitation in sizes 10 and 12. It is killing fished dead-drift or with a deliberate retrieve. Weighted nymphs work well in deeper pools and runs.

The dun stage is known to anglers as the Dark Hendrickson or Black Quill. It emerges at about two o'clock in the afternoon and is sporadically present for the remainder of the day.

Male Subimago or Dun

Tails—three-eighths inch, tannish grey
Body—dark blackish brown, three-eighths inch
Legs—dark blackish brown
Thorax—dark brown
Eyes—large and blackish
Wings—seven-sixteenths inch, dark greyish brown

Female—Subimago or Dun

Tails—center three-eighths inch, outer five-eighths inch, tannish grey
Body—one-half inch, brownish becoming darker at the rear and paler greyish brown underneath
Legs—dark brownish
Thorax—brown
Eyes—small and greyish
Wings—nine-sixteenths inch, greyish brown

The Black Quill is an excellent male imitation in size 14. The Whirling Dun is my favorite for imitating the female subimago, in size 12.

About two days after the duns have hatched, the mature spinners reappear over the water in the nuptial flight. The eggs are laid in fast water, and the freshly hatched nymphs migrate to their natural slow-water habitat. The spinners assume fair importance as early season trout food.

Male Imago or Spinner

Tails—one-half inch, mottled brownish grey
Body—three-eighths inch, dark brownish
Legs—dark brownish grey

Thorax—rich chestnut brown
Eyes—large and blackish
Wings—seven-sixteenths inch, clear and glassy

Female Imago or Spinner

Tails—center three-eighths inch, outer five-eighths inch, mottled
  greyish brown
Body—one-half inch, brownish ringed with dirty yellowish
  grey at the abdominal segments
Legs—brown with darker markings
Thorax—rich brown
Eyes—small and greyish
Wings—nine-sixteenths inch, clear and glassy, with a tinge
  of brown along the leading edge at the tip

The Black Quill Spinner in size 14 is a good imitation of
the males if one is needed, and the Early Brown Spinner
created by Charles Wetzel is an excellent imitation of the
female imago.

Stream notes show *Leptophlebia cupida* emerging on Eastern
waters from the last of April until late May. Some hatching
has been recorded earlier and later, but the principal
emergence activity occurs in early May.

Leptophlebia cupida is the last of the dark May flies of early
season. The hatches that follow include some pale creamish
tan species that occur well into June, and one pale little May
fly that emerges as late as August. These large *Leptophlebia*
hatches mark a turning point in the weather and the hatches
themselves.

EASTERN MAY FLIES: SPRING SEASON

THE DAYS FOLLOWING early season become more pleasant with each passing week. The violets are gone, and in their place we have the dogwood and the choking fragrance of the honeysuckle. Catskill streams become watery avenues through a giant arboretum, and the earth seems washed clean of winter. Trout have now become conscious of surface food, and the dry-fly man will have his innings. It is a time to take large fish on the fly.

Stenonema vicarium (Family Heptagenidae)

This large greyish brown May fly is one of the most important hatches of the entire season. It is considered by many to be on a par with the big *Ephemera* hatches. Known to the angler as the March Brown or Brown Drake, it is a favorite hatch on many streams. Its large size and daylight emergence make it a blessing to the dry-fly addict.

The nymphs are fast-water dwellers which live among the riffles, runs and pocket water. They can stand a wide range of temperatures and current speeds, and for this reason they are widely distributed. The nymphs migrate to the shallows to emerge. Biologists tell us that these May flies take about a year to complete the life cycle, and that all but four days are spent under water.

The nymphs are large and appealing to the fish, and are present in large numbers on most waters. The genus *Stenonema* is rather recent in its description. Insects falling into this genus have a threadlike seventh gill in the nymphal stage. The generic name is descriptive of this characteristic.

Nymphs have dark brownish wing cases with a dark brownish grey thorax. The abdomen is creamish grey heavily banded with dark brown, and the gills are a mottled brownish tan. The legs are tannish grey with brown bands on each femur. The naturals are approximately one-half inch in length. An excellent imitation is the Dark Stenonema Nymph in sizes 10 and 12.

The period of time taken by this insect to escape the nymphal shuck is extremely long, being about twenty seconds. During this time the nymph wriggles along just underneath the surface for several yards. Artificial nymphs are deadly at such times,

Stenonema Nymph

but I also tie a pattern intended to imitate a partially emerged dun. This wet-fly pattern I have named the Emerging March Brown, and it is killing in sizes 10 and 12.

The duns are quite clumsy after they have finally escaped the nymphal skin, and they ride the current for some time before finally getting off, often making several abortive attempts at flight. This fluttering on the surface excites even the most sluggish old lunker, and surface rises to this hatch are sometimes savage.

Male Subimago or Dun

Tails—one-half inch, mottled brownish
Body—one-half inch, creamish tan banded with rich brownish grey on the back segments

Legs—tannish with brown band on each femur
Thorax—mottled brown, cream underneath
Eyes—reddish brown and large
Wings—five-eighths inch, greyish brown with darker brownish
 vein-mottlings

Female Subimago or Dun

Tails—one-half inch, mottled brownish
 Body—nine-sixteenths inch, creamish tan banded with dark
 brown on the back segments
Legs—tannish with brown band on each femur
Thorax—mottled brown, cream underneath
Eyes—small and brownish
Wings—five-eighths inch, greyish brown with darker brownish
 vein-mottlings

The pattern that I use to imitate these male and female duns
is the American March Brown dry fly created by Preston
Jennings. It is most effective in sizes 10 and 12.

One bright afternoon along the Beaverkill, in a little wooded
glade, I had six of these duns resting and moulting on the
hood of my car. They sat very quietly, allowing me to sketch
them and even pick them up for closer scrutiny. Toward the
end of my sketching, when the trout were beginning to rise in
Ferdon's Pool, one of them split the subimago skin and stepped
out with the bright glassy wings of the spinner.

Male Imago or Spinner

Tails—three-quarters inch, mottled brown
Body—one-half inch, greyish cream banded with rich brown-
 ish grey
Legs—brownish tan banded with brown
Thorax—brownish mottled, cream underneath
Eyes—large and reddish brown
Wings—one-half inch, clear and glassy with brown mottlings
 near the tips

Female Imago or Spinner

Tails—one-half inch, mottled brown
 Body—nine-sixteenths inch, creamish tan banded with
 medium brown on the back segments

Legs—tannish banded with brown on each femur
Thorax—tannish flecked with brown
Eyes—small and brownish grey
Wings—five-eighths inch, clear and glassy, with a touch of
brown near the tips

The Great Red Spinner pattern recommended by Charles
Wetzel in his book *Practical Fly Fishing* is an excellent imago
imitation in sizes 10 and 12. The moulting period lasts for
about a day, and the spinners live for about three days. They
may be seen in the evenings, rising and falling over the stream
and riding the current to deposit their eggs.

In thumbing through my stream notes during the preparation of this material, I came across an incident that I cannot
resist describing. It occured on a wonderful blustery day in
the Catskills—a day that produced two beautiful memories,
one of a trout that I landed and killed and one of a trout that
escaped me.

I was on the big water of the Beaverkill and had fished
carefully upstream from Cairns' Pool with very little success.
I succeeded in raising a riffle rainbow or two from the fast
water of Horse Brook Run. As I reached the tail of Hendrickson's Pool a hatch was just beginning. After several minutes of
fishing among the drifting duns, I saw a heavy splash out
along the boulders in deep water, and the brisk wind carried
the spray for several feet. The duns were now all over the
water, and the fish boiled heavily every few moments. Then
two rises came simultaneously, and I realized with a quicken-
ing pulse that there were *two* large fish working instead of one.

The fluttering *Stenonema* duns were being skated across the
surface by the intermittent windy gusts, and the slashing rises
sent tingles through me. I was fascinated by the savage feeding, and watched for several minutes before I realized that I
was not fishing.

The problem at hand was that of getting a decent float
over these fish. Hendrickson's is known for its cut-up cross-
currents, and these fish were well across a main current tongue.

The strong downstream wind helped to drop a beautiful slack curve that produced a two-foot float ending in a heavy splash. The brown wallowed briefly on the surface and then rushed downstream in a run that threatened to take the fight into the fast water below. After some twenty minutes I worked him gently out of the heavy water, and it was all over. Twenty-two inches of glistening hook-jawed brown lay thrashing feebly in the net.

The fish dwarfed my basket so I laid him out in a little side trickle after a firm rap on the head, and returned to the stream. The other fish was still rising noisily. The rises were becoming less frequent now as the hatch was slowing up. I dropped a terrible cast—which I shall blame on the wind, like any true angler—and was sure that I had put the fish down.

Another fluttering subimago was blown across his position and vanished in a vicious splash. He was still feeding as before.

My second attempt fell nicely, and the trout took the fly rather quietly after a four-inch float. The first resistance was not spirited, and I thought that the fish was average in size. Then the temper of the struggle changed as he leaped full length from the water. He was fully as large as the first brown, and he was in a heavy rip now, forcing me to follow him. I cursed the grapefruit-sized rocks in those Beaverkill shallows as I stumbled along in pursuit. One more writhing leap and he was gone.

PLATE TWO: MAY FLIES *(opposite)*

Stenonema canadense male dun; *Stenonema canadense* female dun; *Potamanthus distinctus* male dun; *Potamanthus distinctus* female dun; *Ephemerella walkeri* male dun.

Hexagenia limbata male dun; *Hexagenia limbata* female dun; *Ephemerella needhami* male dun; *Ephemerella needhami* female dun; *Rhithrogena impersonata* male dun.

Stenonema ithaca male dun; *Stenonema ithaca* female dun; *Ephemera varia* male dun; *Ephemera varia* female dun; *Baetis vagans* female dun.

Siphlonurus quebecensis male dun; *Siphlonurus quebecensis* female dun; *Caenis* sp. female dun; *Callibaetis fluctuans* male dun; *Callibaetis fluctuans* female dun.

Heptagenia minerva female dun; *Cinygmula ramaleyi* male dun; *Cinygmula ramaleyi* female dun; *Epeorus nitidus* male dun; *Epeorus nitidus* female dun.

Epeorus longimanus male dun; *Epeorus longimanus* female dun; *Ephemerella infrequens* male dun; *Ephemerella infrequens* female dun; *Baetis* sp. female dun.

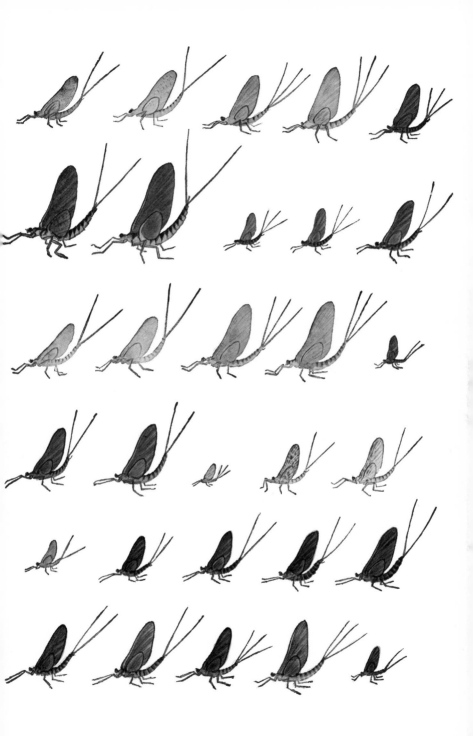

As I reeled in the line there was no disappointment. The windy day was still pleasant as I waded back through the shallows to the big brown on the gravel. I am now glad that I failed to land the second fish, for it left something personal at Hendrickson's. On long winter evenings I like to think that he is still there—a little larger now and far too wise for fumblers like myself. These are the memories that keep one alive during the months between seasons astream.

Stream notes recorded over eight seasons show that *Stenonema vicarium* appears on Pennsylvania and lower New York waters as early as the second week in May. The main hatches occur somewhat later. Good emergence activity may be found farther north as late as the first week in June.

Epeorus vitrea (Family Heptagenidae)

This pale little May fly was formerly classified as *Iron humeralis,* in the subgenus of *Epeorus.* It is important on many Eastern trout streams. The best hatches occur just at twilight during May and June. Anglers know these small May flies as Pale Evening Duns, Pale Watery Duns, Little Marryatts or Little Sulphury Duns.

It emerges from the riffles in late afternoon and early evening, with a concentrated hatch at dusk. The nymph has dark wing cases with a mottled brownish thorax. The abdomen is darkly ringed and greyish tan. The thick little legs are a mottled tannish brown. The tails are long and mottled with brown, like wood-duck flank fibers. The nymph is about one-quarter inch in length. Artificials should be fished dead-drift during much of the season. Since the adult fly escapes his nymphal shuck on the bottom, the nymphs are of little use during actual hatching activity. The Little Marryatt, fished wet, is very deadly during emergence. It should be fished upstream, dead-drift, until it is too dark for such work; then a downstream dead-drift float is deadly. The naturals are extremely active at these times, and trout may be seen working for them in the riffles, below them, and in the shallow tails of pools above large riffles. Fish hit the downstream dead-drift fly very hard at such times.

The Iron Nymph in size 16 is a good imitation of the nymphal stage. It is most effective during low water later in the season. During the emergence, the Little Marryatt tied wet-fly in size 16 is killing.

Duns emerge very quickly from the nymphal skin and move to the surface. They are on the water for a brief moment before taking to the air. For these reasons, their value as a dry-fly prototype is questionable. My notes indicate that the duns usually leave the water as soon as they appear, and the largest fish are not taken on dry-fly imitations.

Male Subimago or Dun

Tails—one-quarter inch, creamish
Body—one-quarter inch, creamish with a very faint olive-yellow tinge and pale tannish bands
Legs—pale creamish with faint tan mottling
Thorax—pale creamish yellow
Eyes—very dark and large
Wings—one-quarter inch, creamish grey

Female Subimago or Dun

Tails—one-quarter inch, creamish
Body—five-sixteenths inch, creamy white with pale tannish markings on the back
Legs—pale creamish with faint mottling
Thorax—pale creamish yellow
Eyes—small and dark greyish
Wings—five-sixteenths inch, creamish grey

The Little Sulphur Dun created by Vincent Marinaro is a useful imitation of the male subimago in size 18. For the females, I like the Pale Watery Dun dressed in size 16. Both of these patterns are excellent.

The spinner stage seems to assume little importance, but in the summer months when hatches are sparse they can be useful as prototypes for imitation. The time lapse between emergence and mating is about two days. These little May flies are commonly found in the spider webs along the banks and under bridges. These spider webs are an excellent guide to what has been hatching from a stream.

Male Imago or Spinner
Tails—three-eighths inch, whitish
Body—one-quarter inch, creamy white with faint brownish markings on the back segments
Legs—creamish tan with faint mottlings
Thorax—creamish, marked with amber
Eyes—very large and dark
Wings—one-quarter inch, glassy clear

Female Imago or Spinner
Tails—one-quarter inch, whitish
Body—five-sixteenths inch, creamish tan with amber back markings
Legs—tannish with amber markings
Thorax—amber
Eyes—small and dark greyish
Wings—five-sixteenths inch, glassy clear

The Pale Watery Spinner in size 18 is an excellent male imitation. The Ginger Quill Spinner in size 16 is a good representation of the female.

Epeorus vitrea emerges sporadically throughout much of the season. It may be found hatching or mating at any time from the middle of May until August. Some evenings produce good activity while others are barren. Notes indicate the best hatches appear in May and June, with emergence concentrated at twilight.

Ephemerella dorothea (Family Baetidae)

This little May fly is quite similar to *Epeorus vitrea* in the dun stage. It is slightly larger and tends to emerge from quieter waters. It is most commonly known to anglers as the Pale Evening Dun and is found emerging from the streams at twilight.

Nymphs of this species are slow-water dwellers, and this is the reason the hatches are most concentrated along the more moderate stretches of current. The nymph is rather small, measuring about three-eighths inch in length. It has dark brownish wing cases, and the thorax is brown. The abdomen is mottled brownish, and the underside of the nymph tends to a paler brownish amber. The legs are brown, and the tails are brownish grey.

The Ephemerella Nymph is an excellent imitation in sizes 14 and 16. These nymphs are best when fished downstream dead-drift during actual twilight emergence activity. While there is light enough to see, the upstream dead-drift technique is killing when fished to rises.

Male Subimago or Dun

Tails—one-quarter inch, greyish cream
Body—one-quarter inch, pale creamy yellow with a faint
   orangish tinge
Legs—pale yellowish grey
Thorax—pale yellowish grey
Eyes—large and dark
Wings—one-quarter inch, pale greyish

Female Subimago or Dun

Tails—one-quarter inch, yellowish white
Body—three-eighths inch, pale yellowish cream
Legs—pale yellowish cream
Thorax—pale yellowish cream
Eyes—small and greyish
Wings—three-eighths inch, very pale greyish

For the males I like a Little Marryatt dressed on a 16 hook. The females are well imitated by the Pale Watery Dun in size 14. These little duns are a great favorite with dry-fly men, for they are easily seen on the water and take several seconds to fly off.

Male Imago or Spinner

Tails—three-eighths inch, yellowish grey
Body—one-quarter inch, pale yellowish tan
Legs—pale yellowish grey
Thorax—pale yellowish grey
Eyes—large and dark

Wings—one-quarter inch, glassy clear

Female Imago or Spinner
Tails—one-quarter inch, yellowish white
Body—three-eighths inch, pale yellowish cream
Legs—pale yellowish cream
Thorax—pale yellowish cream
Eyes—small and greyish
Wings—three-eighths inch, glassy clear
Egg Sac—pale yellowish, at rear of body

This spinner is rather important to anglers, and can be seen mating above the water in clouds. Trout seem to love the egg-filled females if they can get them. They drop their eggs from the air in clusters. However, the flies are so small that a brisk wind can deposit good numbers of them on the water before they can extrude the eggs. The trout are waiting and eager to rise.

My favorite imitations are the Pale Evening Spinner in size 14 for the females and the Male Pale Evening Spinner in a 16 for the males.

Notes taken over nine seasons indicate that *Ephemerella dorothea* emerges and mates from the middle of May until late in June. Streams having the heaviest hatches are of moderate current speeds.

Stenonema fuscum (Family Heptagenidae)

This medium-sized May fly is very important to the Eastern trout fisherman. It is the second important *Stenonema* May fly to emerge. Hatching is rather sporadic throughout the day, making this insect a favorite with dry-fly men. The naturals are known as Ginger Quills on many streams, although some fishermen know them as the Grey Fox hatch. The duns are often present with *Stenonema vicarium,* and the trout seem to be equally fond of the two species.

The nymphs are of the fast-water, clinging variety. They migrate into the shallows to emerge. Average specimens are about one-half inch in length. The wing cases are dark grey, and the thorax is amber mottled with brown. The legs are amber, banded with brown on each femur. The abdomen and gills are amber marked with brown. The tails are mottled like wood-duck flank fibers. The nymphs are very flat. The Stenonema Nymph is a good imitation in size 12.

The subimago flies are quite large and quite similar to the earlier *Stenonema vicarium* species. The wings are sharply slanted to the rear, and the abdomen is turned up more sharply than in other May flies.

Male Subimago or Dun

Tails—seven-sixteenths inch, amber mottled with brown
Body—seven-sixteenths inch, amber with brown markings on the back segments, getting darker toward the rear
Legs—amber with a single brown band on each femur
Thorax—amber mottled with brown
Eyes—large and darkish
Wings—seven-sixteenths inch, glassy grey flecked with slight dark mottlings at the veins

Female Subimago or Dun

Tails—seven-sixteenths inch, amber mottled with brown
Body—one-half inch, amber with light brown markings on the back abdominal segments
Legs—amber banded with brown on each femur
Thorax—amber mottled with brown
Eyes—small and dark
Wings—nine-sixteenths inch, glassy grey flecked with dark mottlings at the veins

The Grey Fox dry fly created by Preston Jennings is an excellent imitation in sizes 12 and 14. It is a pattern to be highly recommended.

Male Imago or Spinner

Tails—eleven-sixteenths inch, greyish amber with dark mottlings like wood-duck flank
Body—seven-sixteenths inch, amber with brownish markings on the back abdominal segments
Legs—amber banded with brown on each femur
Thorax—amber mottled with brown

Eyes—large and dark
Wings—seven-sixteenths inch, glassy clear

Female Imago or Spinner

Tails—seven-sixteenths inch, greyish amber with dark mottlings like wood-duck flank
Body—one-half inch, amber with brownish markings on the back abdominal segments
Legs—amber banded with brown on each femur
Thorax—amber mottled with brown
Eyes—small and dark
Wings—nine-sixteenths inch, glassy clear

The moulting period is about one day, and mating occurs at twilight over the riffles. The imago flies are present for about three days. My favorite imitation of both males and females is the Ginger Quill Spinner in sizes 12 and 14.

This hatch is so common that I have twelve seasons of data on its emergence. Pennsylvania and New Jersey streams have hatches as early as the middle of May. Catskill trout are treated to the hatch in the last days of May, with a few flies emerging well into June. Hatches may occur farther north up to the third week in June.

Paraleptophlebia mollis (Family Baetidae)

This dark little May fly is important in spite of its smallness, and like the earlier hatch of its genus, it causes consternation among the anglers who attempt to match its size and fish the artificials.

This species is well distributed on Eastern trout streams and is most common on the slow stretches. It emerges in late May and June, usually making its daily appearance around eleven o'clock in the morning. The *Paraleptophlebia* hatches are the seasonal Waterloo of most anglers, for without fine tippets and tiny flies an empty basket is assured. It is difficult to play large fish with the diminutive hooks and light tackle too. I know that I have been caught on occasion with nothing smaller than a 16, and have returned to camp and the fly vise with an empty creel.

The nymphs are of the creeping variety. They have a dirty tannish grey thorax with dark wing cases. The abdomens are dark greyish brown with distinct ringing at the segments. The legs are tannish grey, and the tails are tannish brown. The nymphs are about one-quarter inch in length or smaller. The Leptophlebia Nymph in sizes 16 and 18 is an excellent imitation of the naturals.

Male Subimago or Dun

Tails—one-eighth inch, greyish
Body—three-sixteenths inch, greyish ringed
Legs—greyish
Thorax—greyish
Eyes—large and olive-grey
Wings—three-sixteenths inch, dark bluish grey

Female Subimago or Dun

Tails—three-sixteenths inch, greyish
Body—one-quarter inch, greyish ringed
Legs—greyish
Thorax—greyish brown
Eyes—small and greyish
Wings—one-quarter inch, dark bluish grey

The Dark Blue Quill dry fly in sizes 18 and 20 is an excellent imitation. These little duns are known variously as Iron Blue Duns, Iron Blue Quills, Blue Duns, Grey Quills and Blue Quills on various streams of different locale.

Male Imago or Spinner

Tails—three-eighths inch, whitish
Body—three-sixteenths inch, pale whitish with the last two segments a rusty brown
Legs—whitish grey
Thorax—whitish with touches of brown
Eyes—large and reddish brown
Wings—three-sixteenths inch, clear and glassy

Female Imago or Spinner

Tails—one-quarter inch, whitish
Body—one-quarter inch, greyish ringed faintly

Legs—greyish
Thorax—greyish tinged with brown
Eyes—small and dark
Wings—one-quarter inch, glassy clear

The spritely little males are known to anglers as Jenny Spinners, and the Jenny Spinner dry fly in size 20 is an excellent imitation. The females are well imitated by the Blue Quill Spinner in size 18. The mating swarms may be seen rising and falling over the water in the evenings. This species dips its eggs into the water and is of interest to the trout.

Six seasons of data show this May fly to be present from late May until late June. The best hatches seem to occur after eleven o'clock in the morning and last during the midday hours.

Ephemera guttulata (Family Ephemeridae)

This large May fly is considered by many anglers to mark the climax of the Eastern season, and it is awaited with excitement and enthusiasm on many streams. Much of its appeal lies in the fact that extremely large fish often rise during the time when it is on the water.

The flies are known by many local names: shad flies, May flies, Green Mays and other names. The most common name among anglers is Green Drake. The species is scarce on some streams and abundant on others. The Brodhead and Beaverkill have excellent hatches. The Schoharie has a fair hatch, and the Esopus has very sparse hatches. It is rather difficult to isolate a reason for these things, and in many respects *Ephemera guttulata* is a puzzling species.

Two main factors cause the importance of this hatch: the flies are large enough to tempt big trout to the surface, and they hatch in quantities on many waters. They emerge from all parts of the stream and are most abundant on the lower stretches of the rivers—the big water where lunkers are found. The most concentrated emergence comes in the evenings when the larger fish are on the prowl.

The nymphs are of the burrowing variety and live in the detritus and trash that collect on the bottom. They can also live in the silt that lies among the boulders in fast-water streams like the Ausable in New York. Emergence from the nymphal form is quickly accomplished with minnow-like agility.

The standard nymph patterns tied to imitate this species have never proved to be very successful in my trout fishing. Fish that were nymphing steadily during emergence could not be tempted at all. This was always puzzling, and I began to doubt the fact that these nymphs were the pale whitish species commonly described. In the ensuing attempts at collecting a natural I became extremely frustrated. They emerged from their shucks with such speed that I was usually left with an empty shuck and the subimago with which I was already familiar. I began to think that catching the trout was easier than catching the nymphs that the trout were catching.

In my studies of the many nymphal shucks which I did secure, I wondered why the dark tergites of the dun did not show through the thin skin if the natural were whitish as described. Doubt crept into my thinking. Specimens taken from trout in autopsy showed them to be brownish in coloring. This was not conclusive, for the digestive process could have discolored them. About the time that I was going to shelve my studies for the more pleasant task of taking trout, I had an indoor fishing session with Art Flick at Westkill. In the congenial atmosphere of his Westkill Tavern Club, talk finally got around to the Green Drake hatch. He had been puzzled by many of the same peculiarities, and had finally succeeded in capturing one of the elusive nymphs. And it was a dark greyish brown in coloring!

It appears that the pale whitish burrowing nymph described so often is in actuality the nymph stage of another *Ephemera* hatch to be described later.

So the revised description of the nymph must read: wing cases and thorax a greyish brown, legs brownish, gills and abdomen a medium brown, eyes a very dark brown and tails a medium brownish grey. The Dark Ephemera Nymph in sizes 8 and 10 is excellent.

These nymphs spend most of their life cycle in the silt and ooze of the bottom, and trout cannot feed upon them unless high water shifts the silt about. During emergence the nymphs dart quickly to the surface, and rises to them are briskly decisive. Often the largest fish feeding during hatching are never seen at the surface. They are content to take the nymphs under water as soon as they show themselves in the dash for the surface.

Artificials dressed in imitation of this species should have two purposes in mind: deep-fishing after freshets, and retrieve-fishing during a hatch. Weighting will help to get the nymphs down for fishing deep.

Ephemera Nymph

Imitating the duns has always been something of a problem too, for their large size makes them too easily examined by the fish. The dry fly is great sport when the fish are surface-feeding during the hatch. Fast, rough water like the Ausable's West Branch, and long flat pools like those on the Beaverkill, pose some problems. For general purposes the standard dry-fly dressing seems satisfactory, but for very fast water or flat water I like to use a variant dry fly. The variant rides well on the white-water pockets and settles nicely on the flats.

Male Subimago or Dun
Tails—three-quarters inch, olive-brownish
Body—three-quarters inch, creamish grey with a yellowish cast and brown back markings
Legs—creamish grey with a touch of reddish brown on the forelegs
Thorax—yellowish grey touched with brown
Eyes—large and olive-grey

Wings—three-quarters inch, greyish with a faint olive cast and brown mottlings

Female Subimago or Dun

Tails—three-quarters inch, olive-brownish
Body—seven-eighths inch, creamish yellow with dark brownish back markings
Legs—creamish grey with a touch of reddish brown on the forelegs
Thorax—yellowish grey touched with brown
Eyes—small and olive-grey
Wings—seven-eighths inch, greyish olive with brown mottlings

My favorite imitative patterns are the Male Green Drake in size 10 and the Female Green Drake in size 8. The measurements vary widely, with specimens from quiet streams measuring over an inch in the wings. The variant I prefer is the Grey Fox Variant in a size 10; it is not strictly an imitation, but it works well.

Twitching a fly may sound like heresy to the purist, but it is killing during this hatch. The duns are very clumsy and flutter about in their attempts to fly. The occasional twitch of a fluffy variant will often tempt the suspicious browns to rise savagely. Often such fish have learned to refuse motionless flies, and will pass up the natural if it rides passively down the current. The soft, subtle twitch will often spell their demise.

About three days after the duns have hatched, the earliest spinners appear at twilight. First they are high in the air over the stream, dropping lower and lower until the air over the water is filled with them. The transformation is so complete that many anglers do not believe they are the same insect that hatched before. The spinners are known by many local names: Grey Drakes, Grey May Flies and Coffin Flies. The Coffin Flies are so named because of the somber black-and-white coloring of the imago.

Male Imago or Spinner

Tails—one inch, dark brown mottled with black

Body—three-quarters inch, pale yellowish white with slight
brown back markings
Legs—yellowish white with dark reddish brown forelegs
Thorax—yellowish marked with brown
Eyes—large and blackish
Wings—three-quarters inch, glassy but heavily blotched with
deep blackish brown

Female Imago or Spinner

Tails—seven-eighths inch, brown mottled with deep blackish
brown
Body—seven-eighths inch, creamy white with the last segment
a rusty brown
Legs—yellowish white with brown forelegs
Thorax—brownish grey
Eyes—small and dark
Wings—seven-eighths inch, glassy but mottled with dark
brown at the veins

Favorite imitations in my fly box are the Male Coffin Fly
in size 10 and the Female Coffin Fly in size 8. In fast water
such as the Ausable one needs bouyancy and a suggestion of
imitation. I like the White Wulff, tied by Lee Wulff on that
stream in the '20's. It is excellent in sizes 8 and 10.

Trout can waste no time when they feed upon these spinners, for they ride the water briefly to oviposit. Rises are
usually showy and determined, particularly in fast water. Excellent results can be obtained by casting directly to the rises
shortly after a fish has shown himself. The trout seem to bypass drifting spinners as long as the live egg-filled variety are
still in the air.

An eight-season average seems to show *Ephemera guttulata* on
the water from late May in Pennsylvania and New Jersey to
the middle of June in the Adirondacks. The almost unbelievable cloud of naturals, and the spectacular evening rises
of Green Drake time, make some of the most exciting fishing
of the year. And it is a time when the chunky old browns that
rarely fall to anything but minnows or night crawlers can be
deceived with the dry fly. No angler should miss this hatch.

EASTERN MAY FLIES: SUMMER SEASON

By the time that the season is well into June, summer is upon us with all its heat and foliage. The streams are getting low and clear, and the trout feed early and late to escape the heat of midday. Most of the hatches that occur are evening hatches. By the time July has rolled around the fishing is just about over on many Eastern streams. The angler in the Middle West can still enjoy his sport. Water temperatures on some Eastern streams are well into the seventies, and anglers living there must go north or west to continue their sport. The fly-fishing is just beginning in the Rockies.

Isonychia bicolor (Family Baetidae)

This large slate-colored May fly is one of the most important insects of the season, and it seems to have great trout appeal. It may be on the water sporadically from late May until August, even into September—but the best hatches occur in June. It emerges principally in the late afternoon and evening, but dark, cloudy weather sometimes brings a daylight hatch. The nymphs are fast-water dwellers of the swimming type and dart about in the current like tiny minnows.

The nymphs have many interesting characteristics. When

at rest on the fast-water rocks, they hold their forelegs out in front, bracing themselves against the stone with their rear legs and abdomens. These forelegs are fringed with hairs, which serve as a little collecting basket in which plankton and other food is caught.

The nymph is large, measuring about five-eighths inch in length. The general coloring is dark greyish brown. The wing cases are more prominently humped than in the other May fly species, and the three tails are heavily fringed with little hairlike filaments. This fringe of hair is found only on the inside of the outer tails. The eyes are quite prominent and are a dark shiny black. The imitation is the Isonychia Nymph in sizes 10 and 12.

Isonychia Nymph

The nymphs migrate to the shallows to emerge, and crawl out upon the rocks like stone flies. Trout follow them into the shallows to feed. Empty nymphal skins are common on the rocks along the stream. The most effective method of fishing the artificial nymph during hatching is to cast along the banks, giving the nymph an occasional series of gentle twitches suggestive of the swimming action of the naturals as they move about in the current.

The duns are not readily available to the trout, since they split the nymphal skin and emerge out of the water. But enough of them are over the water, or blown into it, to make a dry-fly imitation effective much of the time. It is exciting to hook large fish in the shallow water of the stream.

Male Subimago or Dun
Tails—three-eighths inch, greyish yellow
Body—one-half inch, dark ruddy brown
Legs—forelegs brownish, rear legs cream
Thorax—dark brownish grey
Eyes—large and dark
Wings—nine-sixteenths inch, dark bluish grey

Female Subimago or Dun
Tails—seven-sixteenths inch, greyish yellow
Body—five-eighths inch, dark ruddy brown
Legs—forelegs brownish, rear legs cream
Thorax—dark brownish grey
Eyes—small and dark
Wings—eleven-sixteenths inch, dark bluish grey

When at rest, the duns assume the attitude of the nymph. The forelegs are extended and the dun is supported by the rear legs. The duns are known in various regions as the Leadwing Coachman or Slate Drake. The wet-fly pattern known as the Leadwing Coachman has become rather popular for fishing during this hatch. The method used is fishing the wet fly in the shallows. I believe it is taken by the trout because of its general dark coloring, but it is also refused by some fish. I am convinced that it is successful because it is a rough imitation, but the imitation is not close enough for choosy fish. Since this species emerges out of the water, it is doubtful that the Leadwing is taken as a dun. My conviction that it is refused by choosy trout because it is not a very good imitation is borne out by the success of the Isonychia Nymph.

Since the duns are found emerging in shallow water, a fly that lands softly is an asset. My favorite dry-fly imitation is a big variant that Jeff Norton christened the Grey Variant on the Esopus in 1952. It is deadly during the *Isonychia* activity and has also proved its worth as a fast-water attractor fly when no rises are seen. I use it in sizes 10 and 12.

Male Imago or Spinner
Tails—three-quarters inch, greyish cream
Body—one-half inch, dark rusty reddish brown
Legs—forelegs reddish brown, rear legs cream
Thorax—reddish brown
Eyes—large and blackish
Wings—nine-sixteenths inch, glassy clear

Female Imago or Spinner

Tails—one-half inch, greyish cream
Body—five-eighths inch, fiery brown
Legs—forelegs brown with white feet, rear legs cream
Thorax—reddish brown
Eyes—small and blackish
Wings—eleven-sixteenths inch, glassy clear

The female spinner is the insect that anglers know as the White-Gloved Howdy, named for its little white front feet in the attitude of handshaking. The pattern tied by Charles Wetzel and christened the White-Gloved Howdy is an excellent spinner imitation in sizes 10 and 12.

Stream notes show this May fly on the water from late May until August. Most of the heavy hatches occur at twilight in June. According to Art Flick, these are the best big-trout hatches of the season on the Schoharie.

Hexagenia recurvata (Family Ephemeridae)

This large May fly is the earliest of its genus to emerge on the streams of my acquaintance, and it is often found on the placid limestone waters of Pennsylvania as early as late May. In other streams and lakes farther north, it is found in June and July. The May flies of this genus are the largest found on American waters, and the species which emerge on Middle Western rivers are enormous.

Hexagenia Nymph

The nymphs of this genus are of the burrowing type and live in the silt beds. This restricts them to slow waters having boggy bottoms, or to the silt in the quiet backwaters of the stream. They are easily distinguished from the burrowing

Ephemera nymphs by their anatomy about the head. Full-grown nymphs often measure as much as one inch or more in length.

The nymph has blackish brown wing cases and a dark greyish brown thorax. The abdomen is greyish with brownish back markings and greyish gills. The legs are thick and greyish brown. The hairy tails are greyish. The general appearance is much flatter and heavier than that of the *Ephemera* genus. My favorite imitation is the Hexagenia Nymph in sizes 8 and 10 with a 2X long shank. It should be fished with a swimming, twitching retrieve.

The subimago flies are known as Dark Green Drakes, May Flies, Drake Flies and Drakes. The hatch is rather important on many trout ponds, and on such waters they are also known as Lake Flies. Hatches are often in good numbers, and mating flights take place in clouds. I have collected the moulting duns by the dozens from windows and screens that were near a light after dark.

Male Subimago or Dun

Tails—five-eighths inch, dark mottled brown
Body—five-eighths inch, yellowish brown with dark brown marking at the back segments
Legs—yellowish brown
Thorax—brownish mottled
Eyes—large and dark
Wings—five-eighths inch, dark olive-grey mottled with dark brown

Female Subimago or Dun

Tails—eleven-sixteenths inch, dark mottled brown
Body—three-quarters inch, yellowish brown with dark brown markings at the back segments
Legs—yellowish brown
Thorax—brownish mottled
Eyes—small and dark
Wings—three-quarters inch, dark olive-greyish

My favorite imitation is a modified dressing of the Dark Green Drake tied by Charles Wetzel. I tie it in sizes 8 and 10.

Male Imago or Spinner

Tails—one and three-quarters inches, dark mottled brown
Body—five-eighths inch, rich reddish brown ringed with
  yellowish grey at the segments
Legs—brownish
Thorax—dark reddish brown
Eyes—large and blackish
Wings—five-eighths inch, glassy with heavy mottlings of deep
  reddish brown

Female Imago or Spinner

Tails—one inch, dark mottled brown
Body—three-quarters inch, reddish brown ringed with yellow
Legs—dark brownish
Thorax—brownish
Eyes—small and dark
Wings—three-quarters inch, glassy marked with brown

These spinners are known to anglers as Brown Drakes on
many streams and lakes. My favorite imitation is the Brown
Drake created by Charles Wetzel. I tie and fish a slightly
modified version in sizes 8 and 10. Although these flies are not
on the water for any great length of time, large trout may be
taken in good numbers when they are present. Notes indicate
that they are found sporadically from late May until late July,
with hatches on any one stream or lake lasting about five days.

Ephemerella attenuata (Family Baetidae)

This little olive-bodied May fly is quite important on many
Eastern streams. It hatches in good numbers during the day,
and is usually found on the water during the month of June.
I have long called the natural a Blue-Winged Olive Dun, a
name borrowed from our British colleagues, and the name is
quite appropriate for the dun.

The nymph is rather typical of the genus, with its dark
greyish wing cases and brownish grey thorax, the thin brownish legs, brownish grey abdomen and three short brown-
mottled tails. It is about three-eighths inch in length and is

found primarily in quiet currents. The Dark Ephemerella Nymph in sizes 14 and 16 is an excellent imitation.

Male Subimago or Dun
Tails—one-eighth inch, greyish
Body—one-quarter inch, pale olive-yellow
Legs—greyish
Thorax—olive-brownish
Eyes—large and reddish brown
Wings—one-quarter inch, dark bluish grey

Female Subimago or Dun
Tails—three-sixteenths inch, greyish
Body—five-sixteenths inch, pale olive-yellow
Legs—greyish
Thorax—olive-brownish
Eyes—small and olive-brown
Wings—five-sixteenths inch, dark bluish grey

The little Blue-Winged Olive Dun is an excellent imitation of the males in size 16. The females are well imitated by a size 14.

I first encountered this May fly near the headwaters of Michigan's Pere Marquette, and for several years I thought it was a local species. A few seasons later I encountered an early-morning hatch on the Schoharie in New York. I had been fishing the Esopus the evening before and was on my way to the Ausable after an early start. I found the hatch by accident, for I stopped in the meadow below Lexington just to look at the stream. What I saw caused a blood-pressure rise.

The surface of the pool was covered with these little duns and rising trout. The fish were not small in any man's opinion. I watched a pair of two-pound browns working methodically near the bank for some time. The most amazing thing was the time of half past five!

With nervous, clumsy hands that bungled the stringing of the rod several times—was it the early morning chill that caused the trembling?—I quickly assembled my battle gear. I carefully caught six naturals before I started to fish. It took a great deal of will power.

I would prefer to forget the rest of the story, but I must continue. I caught no trout for one hour while the browns rolled steadily all around me. It was ten minutes and one two-pounder before the hatch was over that I discovered they were nymphing. I reeled in my line and put away my gear, thoroughly humbled at my stupidity.

Male Imago or Spinner

Tails—three-eighths inch, greyish
Body—one-quarter inch, greyish and lightly ringed at the abdominal segments
Legs—greyish
Thorax—greyish tinged with brown
Eyes—large and dark olive-brownish
Wings—one-quarter inch, glassy clear

Female Imago or Spinner

Tails—one-quarter inch, greyish
Body—five-sixteenths inch, greyish ringed at the abdominal segments, faint olive-yellow cast
Legs—greyish
Thorax—greyish tinged with brown
Eyes—small and olive-brown
Wings—five-sixteenths inch, glassy clear

These little imago flies have never been too important in my experience with the hatches, but the Blue Quill Spinner is a good imitation in size 16 if one is needed. Six seasons of notes show these May flies to be present during the last three weeks in June.

Leptophlebia johnsoni (Family Baetidae)

This greyish little May fly emerges on Eastern streams during the month of June. It is quite similar to the *Paraleptophlebia* hatches, which precede it in the emergence cycle, but it is slightly larger in size.

The nymph ranges about freely on the bottom, and it is a common trout food. It measures about three-eighths inch in length. The wing cases are dark greyish brown, and the thorax is greyish with a faint orangish cast. The legs and tails are brownish tan. The body is yellowish brown and the eyes are very dark. The Pale Leptophlebia Nymph in sizes 14 and 16 is a good imitation. It should be fished dead-drift most of the time.

Male Subimago or Dun

Tails—one-quarter inch, brownish grey
Body—one-quarter inch, brownish olive
Legs—brownish grey
Thorax—brownish
Eyes—large and dark
Wings—five-sixteenths inch, very dark bluish grey

Female Subimago or Dun

Tails—five-sixteenths inch, brownish grey
Body—five-sixteenths inch, olive-brownish
Legs—brownish
Thorax—brownish
Eyes—small and dark
Wings—three-eighths inch, very dark bluish grey

My favorite imitation is the well-known Iron Blue Dun in sizes 14 and 16. This stage lasts about four days before the final moulting takes place. These little duns are quite important on many streams.

Male Imago or Spinner

Tails—five-eighths inch, mottled whitish
Body—one-quarter inch, whitish with the last two segments
    bright reddish brown
Legs—brown
Thorax—reddish brown
Eyes—large and dark
Wings—five-sixteenths inch, glassy clear

Female Imago or Spinner

Tails—seven-eighths inch, greyish white
Body—five-sixteenths inch, pale greyish faintly ringed at the abdominal segments
Legs—brownish
Thorax—brownish grey
Eyes—small and dark
Wings—three-eighths inch, clear and glassy

The males are rather well imitated by the familar Jenny Spinner in size 16. I prefer the Blue Quill Spinner in size 14 for the female representation. One may find this species on the water in late May and June.

Ephemerella needhami (Family Baetidae)

This ruddy-bodied little May fly is often found on the water with the earlier *attenuata* species of this slow-water genus. It never seems to be as important as that larger species. Perhaps the trout prefer *attenuata* because it is more of a mouthful.

The nymphs have the typical brownish grey appearance of this genus. They measure about one-quarter inch in length. The Dark Ephemerella Nymph in a size 16, fished dead-drift, is an excellent imitation.

Male Subimago or Dun

Tails—one-eighth inch, greyish
Body—one-quarter inch, ruddy brownish
Legs—greyish
Thorax—greyish brown
Eyes—rusty brown
Wings—one-quarter inch, dark bluish grey

Female Subimago or Dun

Tails—one-quarter inch, greyish
Body—five-sixteenths inch, ruddy brownish
Legs—greyish
Thorax—greyish brown
Eyes—rusty brown
Wings—five-sixteenths inch, bluish grey

These little duns are well imitated by the Red Quill in sizes 16 and 18. The hatching activity is concentrated around eleven o'clock in the morning and lasts about one hour.

Male Imago or Spinner
Tails—five-sixteenths inch, mottled greyish
Body—one-quarter inch, brownish ringed
Legs—greyish brown
Thorax—brownish
Eyes—rusty red
Wings—one-quarter inch, glassy clear

Female Imago or Spinner
Tails—one-quarter inch, mottled greyish
Body—five-sixteenths inch, brownish ringed
Legs—greyish brown
Thorax—brownish
Eyes—small and brownish
Wings—five-sixteenths inch, glassy clear

The Little Rusty Spinner is an excellent imitation of the males in size 18, and of the females in a size 16. Mating occurs during the late afternoon and evening hours.

This hatch is rarely important by itself, although some individual fish may be feeding upon the flies. One exception to this occurred on the Little South Pere Marquette. I was fishing this pleasant stream on the lovely wooded stretch above Powers' Bridge with Gerry Queen, an angling friend from Detroit who knows that Michigan country well. It was a wonderful morning, with a sky of indescribable blue and big, clean-looking cumulus clouds, and the water was sparkling and alive. You have seen the water with that lively look; you have also seen it dead and uninviting in a way that dampens the enthusiasm the moment you wade out into the current. Not many fish were rising to the naturals, but each likely pocket under the willows or beside a log seemed to produce a rise. The fish took the fly quietly in these still flats. Gerry stopped fishing and relaxed under a tree as I kept at it. The ten or twelve browns that I caught and released were not large, but I was happy with them.

Under a long stretch of shaded bend my tiny Little Red Quill disappeared in a lazy dimple. I struck, and a large fish rolled in the shallows. He was at least twenty inches long; and it was a very brief cat-and-mouse struggle, with myself in the rodent's role. The fragile leader parted, and the fish swam downstream through the quiet, waist-deep water into a deep hole. He was in plain sight as he passed casually and without alarm. Apparently it had all happened before. I had never seen a fish of that size on that water, and I have not had the opportunity to fish in Michigan since.

Stenonema canadense (Family Heptagenidae)

This pale creamish May fly makes one of the most important summer hatches. It is found primarily during late June and early July. Hatching is sporadic throughout the day, with the heaviest concentrations at twilight. Although there are many pale May flies on the water in this part of the season, the large *Stenonema* flies seem to be more attractive than the others.

The nymphs are fast-water dwellers and are quite similar to the nymphs of the earlier *Stenonema* flies. Naturals are about one-half inch in length. The Stenonema Nymph in sizes 12 and 14 is excellent as an imitation.

Male Subimago or Dun

Tails—three-eighths inch, pale mottled tan
Body—three-eighths inch, mottled tannish with faint brown back markings
Legs—tannish banded faintly with brown
Thorax—tannish
Eyes—large and blackish
Wings—three-eighths inch, mottled creamish tan

Female Subimago or Dun

Tails—seven-sixteenths inch, pale mottled tan
Body—seven-sixteenths inch, mottled tannish with faint brown back markings

Legs—tannish banded faintly with brown
Thorax—tannish
Eyes—small and dark
Wings—one-half inch, mottled creamish tan

The well-loved Light Cahill is as fine an imitation as one can find in sizes 12 and 14. It was first tied by Theodore Gordon as a variation of the original Cahill tied by Dan Cahill of Port Jervis, New York. The very pale dressing now in vogue was created by William Chandler on the famous Neversink. As the Light Cahill was the pattern on which I caught my first large fish, a brown of eighteen inches, I am especially fond of it.

Male Imago or Spinner

Tails—five-eighths inch, mottled tannish
Body—three-eighths inch, tannish with faint brown markings on the back
Legs—tannish banded with brown on each femur
Thorax—tannish
Eyes—large and blackish
Wings—three-eighths inch, glassy clear

Female Imago or Spinner

Tails—one-half inch, mottled tannish
Body—seven-sixteenths inch, tannish with faint brown back markings and a pinkish cast
Legs—tannish banded with light brown
Thorax—tannish
Eyes—small and dark
Wings—one-half inch, glassy clear

These spinners ride the water to oviposit and are present for about two days. For these reasons they are rather important. The Ginger Quill Spinner in size 14 is an excellent male imitation. The Little Salmon Spinner in size 12 imitates the females.

Stream data indicate that these May flies appear in the middle of June and may be on the water until July. They hatch throughout the day, but the heaviest hatching occurs at twilight. It is an excellent dry-fly hatch.

Hexagenia limbata (Family Ephemeridae)

This large, juicy May fly makes up the fantastic and erroneously named "caddis" hatches in the Midwest. In reality this "caddis" hatch is a heavy mating flight of large May flies. Hatching occurs from twilight until about eleven o'clock. Mating comes at the same times, but trout may pick up the spent flies into the early morning hours. Night fishing at this time produces many heavy fish.

The hatches have long been a point of controversy among Michigan anglers, with one group sticking to the name "caddis hatch" and another maintaining that it is a May fly hatch and should be called such. Having been reared as a trout fisherman on Michigan streams, I long knew the hatches as caddis hatches. But my insect collecting revealed things that deflated tradition. There were few real caddis flies present during these hatches. Most of the insects in the air and on the water seemed to be *Hexagenia limbata* May flies. They appeared by the thousands.

The misnomer may have started when Art Winnie, the old Michigan night-fishing maestro, began tying a big dry fly for night fishing. He named the fly the Michigan Night Caddis for lack of a better name, and "caddis" took root for both the fly and the night hatches. This was many years ago, and the name still persists.

The nymphs are of the burrowing type and measure as much as one and one-half inches in length. They are most common in quiet streams with large silt beds along the banks. The nymphs have dark greyish brown wing cases, a greyish brown thorax, greyish bodies with brownish back markings, greyish gills and three hairy greyish tails. The Hexagenia Nymph is an excellent imitation in sizes 8 and 6. The hooks used should have 3X long shanks.

Male Subimago or Dun

Tails—one-half inch, mottled dark grey
Body—three-quarters inch, greyish, marked on the back and belly with brown diamond-shaped marks
Legs—greyish tan
Thorax—greyish mottled with brown
Eyes—large and dark
Wings—three-quarters inch, dark bluish grey

Female Subimago or Dun

Tails—seven-eighths inch, dark mottled grey
Body—one and one-quarter inches, yellowish grey marked with brown diamond markings
Legs—greyish tan
Thorax—yellowish grey mottled with brown
Eyes—small and dark
Wings—one and one-half inches, bluish grey

The males are well imitated by the Dark Michigan Mayfly in size 8; females by the Light Michigan Mayfly in size 6.

The duns usually emerge just at twilight and continue to hatch until about eleven o'clock, but some individuals make their appearance during the day. The heaviest activity seems to come between nine and ten, but this is only a general rule. Experienced anglers can almost feel a hatch in the air, and can follow the peak of the hatch as it progresses upstream. According to one local angler I met on the Baldwin, the best nights are "dark as the inside o' yer hat; sorta warm an' muggy." He had three browns over seventeen inches.

Male Imago or Spinner

Tails—one and one-half inches, mottled grey
Body—three-quarters inch, creamish yellow with brown diamond back markings
Legs—yellowish
Thorax—yellowish mottled with brown
Eyes—large and dark
Wings—three-quarters inch, glassy clear

Female Imago or Spinner

Tails—seven-eighths inch, mottled grey
Body—one and one-quarter inches, yellowish with brown
diamond-shaped markings
Legs—yellowish
Thorax—yellowish mottled with brown
Eyes—small and dark
Wings—one and one-half inches, glassy clear

The Michigan Spinner is my favorite pattern for this mating flight in sizes 6 and 8. It has produced several very large fish for me in the past.

I have often fished Michigan streams during this hatch, following the activity north from the Pere Marquette to the Boardman and up. I have not fished these streams for several years now, but each year at the end of June I am fishing the May fly hatch in thought. It is a time for lunkers on the dry fly, and my best night-fishing brown went twenty-five inches.

The first time that I witnessed the rise I was without tackle. Such things are common—one never has a gun when the biggest buck shows himself, or the camera is without film when the wildest-leaping rainbow of the trip is hooked and landed. I had stopped along the Pere Marquette at twilight just to pay my homage. It was already so dark that I did not expect to see anything. I could hear the river below and see the pines silhouetted downstream. Cars droned by on the busy highway, but as they passed and it became quiet, I could hear another sound. The fish were rising all over the stream. The big browns under the bridge, which I had never seen before, went wild in an orgy of feeding. It did not last very long, and the river was quiet again. I could hear a fisherman wading the shallows toward the bridge, so I waited to see how he had done. It was an evening to remember; he had three fish over two pounds.

Many local flies are tied to imitate or fish this hatch, and all of them work fairly well. Still there are times when the fish discriminate against their un-May-fly-like shapes and a real imitation is needed. Then one must have the May fly silhouette and coloring. The fly patterns described in this section were the result of several seasons' experimentation. The naturals were carefully considered in the process, and the balance between imitation and the floating qualities needed was worked out.

The local anglers often use flies as large as size 4 on the big night-feeders. Anglers from other regions are frequently amazed at these monstrosities. There are many scoffers too, but perhaps these big flies could be put to good use on brown-trout streams elsewhere. At any rate, the swish-swish of big flies in the night is a common sound on Michigan streams in late June and July.

Night fishing can get into your blood, and your senses become amazingly attuned to it. You will find yourself casting accurately to rises that you only hear. The slightest disturbance near your fly puts the reflex on edge; you must strike at these rises, for it is easy to assume your fly to be elsewhere and never strike at a good fish. The leader should be tapered to 1X or heavier, for one must strike a big fish hard and often play him hard. Too many times I have had a hook rake the teeth of a big brown because my strike was too soft. And one cannot let the fish range too freely among the unseen snags. Fishing the May fly hatches in the Midwest is fantastic. It leads to exaggeration and apoplexy, and also produces fish up to ten pounds for those who know how.

A word of caution—never fish any stream at night without knowing its bottom well. It can be dangerous as well as thrilling. No true angler can afford to miss the fun, but he should learn the water carefully in the daylight before trying the after-hours stuff.

Stenonema ithaca (Family Heptagenidae)

This pale little May fly is quite similar to *Stenonema canadense* in the dun stage. The spinner lacks the pinkish cast found in the abdominal segments of the earlier female imago flies. It emerges from the shallows in late afternoon and early evening. Both pale May flies of this genus often emerge together.

Nymphs of both species are very nearly identical, with the nymph of *ithaca* tending to be slightly darker in cast than that of *canadense*. The nymph is about seven-sixteenths inch in length and is well imitated by the Stenonema Nymph in sizes 12 and 14.

Male Subimago or Dun

Tails—five-sixteenths inch, mottled tannish
Body—five-sixteenths inch, tannish with faint brown markings
   on the back segments
Legs—tannish banded with brown on each femur
Thorax—tannish mottled faintly with brown
Eyes—large and dark
Wings—three-eighths inch, mottled creamish grey

Female Subimago or Dun

Tails—seven-sixteenths inch, mottled tannish
Body—seven-sixteenths inch, tannish with faint brown mark-
   ings on the back segments
Legs—tannish banded with brown
Thorax—tannish mottled faintly with brown
Eyes—small and dark
Wings—one-half inch, mottled creamish

The Light Cahill in sizes 12 and 14 is an excellent imitation of these duns. These hatches are important on most Eastern streams, where they emerge in good numbers during the last two weeks in June.

Male Imago or Spinner

Tails—five-eighths inch, mottled tannish
Body—five-sixteenths inch, tannish marked with light brown
   on the back segments
Legs—tannish banded with brown
Thorax—tannish mottled with brown
Eyes—large and dark
Wings—three-eighths inch, glassy clear

Female Imago or Spinner

Tails—one-half inch, mottled tannish
Body—seven-sixteenths inch, tannish marked with light
  brown on the back segments
Legs—tannish banded with brown at the tergites
Thorax—tannish mottled with brown
Eyes—small and dark
Wings—one-half inch, glassy clear

These spinners are rather important as they ride the water
to oviposit. They mate in the late afternoon and evening over
the riffles and runs. The Ginger Quill Spinner imitates them
well in sizes 12 and 14. The spinners may often be seen together in copula over the water, sometimes falling into the
stream. An alert trout can frequently capture two May flies in
one rise.

Potamanthus distinctus (Family Ephemeridae)

These pale May flies hatch just at twilight on Eastern trout
streams, and are present in late June and July. They are of

*Potamanthus
Nymph*

the burrowing type, and the nymphs are found
in quiet water or eddies of the faster water. They
are sometimes found in the trash under stones in
the more quiet riffles and runs. Among many
local names for these May flies are Golden Drake,
Cream Dun, Evening Dun and Golden Spinner.

The nymphs measure about five-eighths inch in
length and are rather dark in general coloring.
The thorax and wing cases are a very dark reddish
brown, the abdomen is reddish brown with
brownish gills, the legs are mottled brownish, and
the three tails are brownish. The Potamanthus
Nymph in sizes 12 and 14 is killing.

Male Subimago or Dun

Tails—one-half inch, yellowish
Body—one-half inch, yellowish cream with faint brownish
  markings on the back segments

Legs—yellowish cream
Thorax—yellowish cream
Eyes—large and dark
Wings—one-half inch, creamish

Female Subimago or Dun

Tails—five-eighths inch, yellowish
Body—five-eighths inch, yellowish cream with faint orangish
  brown back markings
Legs—yellowish cream
Thorax—yellowish cream
Eyes—small and dark
Wings—five-eighths inch, creamish yellow

The duns are well imitated by the little-known Paulinskill
dry fly, created by Ray Bergman. It is best tied in sizes 10 and
12 for this hatch. Since the hatches are often found when the
streams are very low, many anglers prefer a Cream Variant in
size 12, for the soft way it drops to the surface of a shallow flat.

Male Imago or Spinner

Tails—three-quarters inch, yellowish mottled
Body—one-half inch, pale yellowish
Legs—yellow with reddish forelegs and yellow feet
Thorax—yellowish, reddish median stripe dorsally
Eyes—large and dark
Wings—one-half inch, glassy with blotches of faint yellow at
  the leading edges

Female Imago or Spinner

Tails—three-quarters inch, yellowish mottled
Body—five-eighths inch, pale yellowish
Legs—yellow with reddish forelegs and yellow feet
Thorax—yellowish, median dorsal stripe of red
Eyes—small and dark
Wings—five-eighths inch, glassy tinged with yellow

My favorite imitation is the Golden Spinner in sizes 10 and
12. These spinners mate at twilight and continue the nuptial
flight well after dark. I have raised some large fish after dark
with an imitation.

These May flies often emerge when the water temperatures are too high for much trout activity. I have seen them hatching in the Beaverkill with the water hovering around seventy-eight degrees. There were no rises seen. Emergence is quick and minnow-like, with the duns popping out abruptly on the surface. They ride the water for some time before flying off to the brush. Good rises of trout will occur if the streams are not too warm.

Ephemera varia (Family Ephemeridae)

This hatch of pale yellowish May flies is known to anglers as the Yellow May or Yellow Drake hatch. It is common on Eastern trout waters in July, with the best hatches occuring at twilight. It is quite similar to the earlier hatch of its genus, except that it is much paler both as a nymph and as an adult.

The nymph measures about three-quarters inch in length. The wing cases are greyish with a pale creamish thorax. The legs, abdomen, tails and gills are cream. The eyes are small and darkish. The Ephemera Nymph in sizes 10 and 12 is an effective imitation.

Male Subimago or Dun

Tails—five-eighths inch, tannish mottled
Body—one-half inch, pale yellowish cream with faint back markings at the segments
Legs—creamy white, brownish forelegs
Thorax—yellowish cream
Eyes—large and dark
Wings—one-half inch, creamish faintly marked with brown in the manner of its genus

Female Subimago or Dun

Tails—five-eighths inch, tannish mottled
Body—five-eighths inch, pale yellowish cream faintly marked with brown on the back segments
Legs—creamish white, brown forelegs
Thorax—creamish yellow
Eyes—small and dark

Wings—eleven-sixteenths inch, glassy tinged with a faint yellowish cast and brownish mottlings

The Paulinskill dry fly in sizes 10 and 12 and the Cream Variant in size 12 work as well for this hatch as for the *Potamanthus* flies. The two May fly species are often present together.

Male Imago or Spinner

Tails—one inch, yellowish marked with brown
Body—one-half inch, creamish yellow with dark brown back markings
Legs—creamish yellow, forelegs brownish
Thorax—yellowish brown
Eyes—large and dark
Wings—one-half inch, glassy marked with brown

Female Imago or Spinner

Tails—seven-eighths inch, yellow marked with brown
Body—five-eighths inch, yellowish marked with brown on the back segments
Legs—creamish yellow, forelegs brownish
Thorax—yellowish brown
Eyes—small and dark
Wings—eleven-sixteenths inch, glassy with a faint yellowish tinge and brownish mottlings

The Yellow Drake in sizes 10 and 12 is an excellent imitation of the spinners. The naturals appear about two days after the duns have hatched, and mate over the riffles. They ride the water to oviposit, and are important as trout food for this reason. In the rising-and-falling nuptial flights, they never rise far from the water. The naturals emerge during July.

Some Less Important Species

There are several species and genera of May flies that are of questionable value to the angler because they so rarely assume any significance as trout food. Stream notes show a few occasions scattered over the seasons when they were briefly of importance for a day or so.

The species *Rhithrogena impersonata* was originally described from Quebec, but it also emerges from the swift trout streams of our north country. It emerges during the early days of June on Adirondack streams. The nymphs are easily recognized by their rusty reddish gills. Except for the gill coloring, the nymphs are quite like those of the genus *Epeorus*. The Rhithrogena Nymph in size 12 is an excellent imitation, if one becomes necessary.

> *Female Subimago or Dun*
> Tails—one-half inch, dark greyish brown
> Body—one-half inch, dark greyish, deeply ringed with rich brownish grey
> Legs—brownish grey
> Thorax—brownish grey
> Eyes—small and dark
> Wings—five-eighths inch, very dark bluish grey

The Dark Gordon Quill in sizes 10 and 12 is an excellent imitation of the *Rhithrogena* duns. The hatches emerge from the fast-water stretches. I have never seen the spinner stage in even moderate quantities, and it has never assumed any importance in my fishing.

One May fly of the genus *Ephemerella* does not achieve the stature of its cousins as a primary trout food. It is known to anglers as the Olive Quill or Olive Dun, and to the entomologists as *Ephemerella walkeri*. An imitation is rarely required, but notes show that when it is needed it is needed badly. It is most commonly found on the very slow-moving streams, and emerges around the end of May and early June.

Ephemerella Nymph, Fuscata Group

The nymphs are small and heavy looking, with a dirty olive-brown appearance. The fat little legs are the only exception to the olive hue, and they are a dirty tannish grey. The insects measure about three-eighths inch in length. The Olive Dun Nymph in size 14 is a good imitation if one is needed.

Female Subimago or Dun
Tails—seven-sixteenths inch, tannish grey
Body—three-eighths inch, deep olive-brown
Legs—tannish grey
Thorax—deep olive-brown
Eyes—small and olive
Wings—seven-sixteenths inch, very dark olive-greyish

The Olive Dun in size 14 is a good imitation when one is needed. Hatching activity occurs sporadically during the daylight hours. The mating spinners are scattered and unimportant as trout food.

There are several May flies of the genus *Siphlonurus* that are of occasional value. They are generally known to anglers as Brown Quills or Brown Quill Spinners. The hatching usually occurs during the afternoon and evening in late May and June. Spinner flights take place in the evening and are occasionally of some importance.

Siphlonurus Nymph

The nymphs are of the swimming variety and are most common in slower streams. The wing cases are brownish grey and the thorax is greyish. The brownish grey body and brownish gills are rather long. The legs are greyish brown. There are three tannish grey tails with dark traverse markings; there are filaments on the inside of the outer tails and on both sides of the middle tail. The tails are used to propel and guide the nymph as it darts about on the bottom in search of food. The Siphlonurus Nymph in sizes 10 and 12 is an excellent imitation.

The species *Siphlonurus quebecensis* is typical of its genus. It is fairly important on some streams, but most waters have several species of this genus present at the same time.

Male Subimago or Dun

Tails—three-eighths inch, greyish brown
Body—one-half inch, greyish ringed with brown
Legs—greyish brown
Thorax—greyish brown
Eyes—large and dark
Wings—one-half inch, greyish brown

My favorite pattern for imitation of these *Siphlonurus* duns is a modified Cahill Quill of mixed dun and light brown hackle tied in sizes 12 and 14. It has worked very well for several seasons when imitations were needed.

Male Imago or Spinner

Tails—one and one-half inches, dark brownish
Body—one-half inch, greyish ringed with brown
Legs—brownish
Thorax—brownish grey
Eyes—large and dark
Wings—one-half inch, glassy clear

Female Imago or Spinner

Tails—one inch, dark yellowish ringed with brown
Body—five-eighths inch, yellowish grey ringed with dark
  reddish brown
Legs—brownish
Thorax—reddish brown
Eyes—small and dark
Wings—five-eighths inch, glassy clear
Egg Sac—pale greenish yellow

The Red Quill Spinner in size 14 is a good representation of the male. The Brown Quill Spinner tied by Charles Wetzel is an excellent imitation of the egg-filled female stage. Mating takes place at twilight on most trout waters during early June. The female imitations should be dressed in size 12.

The little May flies of the genus *Baetis* are numerous on most trout waters and occasionally assume major importance to the angler. They are widely distributed and have more than one brood each season. May flies of this genus produce three broods per year, two of which fall within the trout season. These little flies were sometimes classified under the old generic name *Acentrella*. In general coloring they are dark bluish grey with a faint olive cast to their abdomens. They measure one-quarter inch in the wings and bodies and one-eighth inch in the tails. This seems to be about the maximum size for any species of the genus. The Dark Blue Quill is an excellent imitation of the duns in sizes 16 through 22.

The imago flies are important because they go under water to lay their eggs. For this reason both wet and dry imitations are useful. Male spinners of this genus tend to be pale tannish or brown, and the Ginger Quill Spinner in size 18 is excellent. The females are more reddish brown in coloring, and the Red Quill Spinner in sizes 16 and 18 has proved effective. The spinners have the typical glassy clear wings of the imago.

The nymphs of these May flies can become important trout food in spite of their small size. They move about freely in the fast-water stretches and are very numerous. They vary in coloring in the shades of brown, presenting a mottled appearance. They are slender and fishlike, lacking the thick, humped thorax of other genera. The *Baetis* nymphs measure about one-quarter to three-eighths inch on the average, and tend to be somewhat larger than the adult flies. The Baetis Nymph in sizes 14 and 16 often is a rather valuable pattern.

Caenis Nymph

Other common many-brooded genera are *Caenis* and *Cloeon*, the tiny two-winged May flies. There are several subgenera of these groups, but the distinctions are unimportant to the trout fisherman. All of these insects have only two wings instead of the usual four. These insects hatch and moult as soon as they reach a resting spot. Then the mating dance begins immediately. They are tiny insects, averaging about one-eighth inch in the wings and bodies, and no hook is too small for an imitation.

The nymphs sprawl in the mud and trash of quiet pools

and are extremely numerous. They are about three-sixteenths inch in length and generally greyish. The little Caenis Nymph in size 18 is effective.

Since the moulting from dun to spinner begins almost as the subimago leaves the water, the trout have very little chance at the dun stage. Therefore imitations of the imago form are most desirable. I have found the Caenis dry fly recommended

by Alvin Grove to be very effective, in sizes 18 through 22. The Ginger Quill Spinner is also good in these sizes.

Another many-brooded genus of some importance to the angler is *Callibaetis*. It is found primarily in slow, weedy streams and ponds. The nymph is a crawler that hides and feeds in the vegetation. Flies of this genus complete their life cycle in five to six weeks, and there are two or three

Callibaetis Nymph

generations each season. One can expect hatches in May, July and August on many waters.

Female Subimago or Dun

Tails—one-quarter inch, mottled greyish
Body—one-quarter inch, greyish ringed
Legs—greyish marked at the joints
Thorax—greyish
Eyes—small and grey
Wings—one-quarter inch, greyish heavily mottled with darker
   blotches

Female Imago or Spinner

Tails—three-eighths inch, greyish
Body—one-quarter inch, greyish tan
Legs—greyish marked at the joints
Thorax—greyish tan
Eyes—small and dark
Wings—one-quarter inch, glassy clear with touches of black
   along the leading edges

The Grey Quill dry fly in sizes 16 and 18 is an excellent subimago imitation. The Grey Quill Spinner is a good imitation of the imago in the same sizes. The naturals emerge during the day, and mating seems to take place at twilight. The Callibaetis Nymph in size 16 is of some value.

The little yellowish flies of the genus *Heptagenia* are another common species on Eastern streams. They are rarely of importance, and are being mentioned for purposes of identification by the angler. The duns are quite yellowish in coloring, with large blackish eyes. They are rarely larger than one-quarter inch in the wing and body measurements. These little duns emerge just at twilight, and continue to emerge well after dark. They have faint mottlings along the leading edge of their yellowish wings. The Little Yellow Mayfly is an imitation in sizes 16 and 18, if one is needed.

Stream notes indicate that the genus *Heptagenia* is on the water in its various species during June, July and August. It is rarely of much importance.

WESTERN MAY FLIES: EARLY HATCHES

HATCHING ACTIVITY and the subsequent fly-rod sport come much later on Western waters. When the angler on the Beaverkill is finding clouds of May flies in early June, the Western fisherman is usually confronted with turbulent snow water coming from the high country. Hatches are scattered until the streams clear up and lose their torrential character. In the high parks and valleys of the Rockies, the aspens are just getting a touch of green against the deep rich pines. The first columbines are blooming in the rocky sheltered places, giving hints of the color to come in the high meadows. The midday sun in the valleys is quite warm, but winter chills the air quickly when the sun drops behind the western ranges. The snow still lies draped above the timberline, and is still to surge down the little streams to the valley in the spring runoff.

Because of these conditions, heavy hatching is rarely encountered before late June. Smaller streams, not affected by the snow water because of beaver dams or other reasons, are often exceptions to this rule, and I have recorded scattered hatches on them as early as the first week in June. The clever man with a nymph will score on water that is clear enough for the fly whether the hatches have appeared or not.

Since altitude variations are so pronounced on Western streams, it is almost impossible to give any general rules about when ecdysis will occur. Insects emerge under definite seasonal conditions, and the abrupt altitude drop on individual streams is so great that the hatches are affected. The Frying Pan in Colorado is an excellent example for study. It lies at an altitude of roughly five thousand feet where it joins the Roaring Fork at Basalt. Yet in the headwater meadows it winds in altitudes up to nine thousand feet, and the water is so icy that wading is uncomfortable.

The resulting effect upon the hatches is that insects that have long since disappeared from the lower river have only started to emerge in the high meadows. Flies that are emerging at Ruedi, about half way upstream from Basalt, will be found hatching weeks later in the meadows above Nast. Such things are common when a stream falls four thousand feet in twenty miles.

Since it is so difficult to determine a set cycle of hatches for Western waters, the species discussed have been arranged in a rough chronological order. Compiling the exact sequence of hatches would mean fishing just one stream throughout the season. I lack the persistence to restrict my sport that much; I love so many streams in the Rockies that I could not fish just one.

Much of the material gathered in these pages came from Colorado and Wyoming streams, and much still remains to be done in that country. Every time I fish the Frying Pan, I fully expect that wonderful stream to serve up some species that is completely foreign to me.

Cinygmula ramaleyi (Family Heptagenidae)

This little May fly seems to be the first of the season on many streams, and trout will rise to it if only the water is clear. My principal experiences with it took place on smaller streams at around eight thousand feet. Emergence takes place in the late morning, from the fast water. The flies seem to hatch in both good and bad weather, so it pays to be astream during the time these duns are on the water. This hatch is excellent for satiating a winter-long dry-fly urge.

The nymph is a fast-water dweller measuring about one-quarter inch in length. Its coloring is a dark reddish brown, with greyish wing cases and mottled brownish legs. The flat little nymphs are well equipped for clinging to the fast-water rocks. My favorite imitation is the Cinygmula Nymph in size 16.

Male Subimago or Dun

Tails—one-eighth inch, greyish
Body—one-quarter inch, ruddy brown ringed
Legs—brownish grey
Thorax—brownish
Eyes—large and dark
Wings—one-quarter inch, dark bluish grey

Female Subimago or Dun

Tails—one-eighth inch, greyish
Body—five-sixteenths inch, ruddy brown
Legs—brownish grey
Thorax—brownish grey
Eyes—small and dark
Wings—five-sixteenths inch, bluish grey

Both males and females are imitated well by the Dark Red Quill in sizes 16 and 18. I have taken many fine trout on this pattern during the hatch.

Male Imago or Spinner

Tails—three-eighths inch, greyish white
Body—one-quarter inch, dark reddish brown
Legs—reddish brown
Thorax—reddish brown
Eyes—large and dark
Wings—one-quarter inch, glassy clear

Female Imago or Spinner

Tails—one-quarter inch, greyish white
Body—five-sixteenths inch, reddish brown

Legs—reddish brown
Thorax—reddish brown
Eyes—small and dark
Wings—five-sixteenths inch, glassy clear

These little spinners mate at midday over the riffles and runs. The little Red Quill Spinner is an excellent imitation in sizes 16 and 18. Since many of the spent flies become drowned, a wet-fly imitation is an excellent pattern to carry. Stream notes show these flies to hatch during June.

Epeorus nitidus (Family Heptagenidae)

This large dark May fly is one of the most unusually colored insects to hatch on Western streams, for its sternites are a reddish maroon. It is not a common species and is often found hatching with other May flies. I have found occasional fish selective to these maroon-bellied duns often enough to make them important.

The high-meadow stretches of the Arkansas above Malta, Colorado, have good hatches, which usually appear in late June and early July. They are on the water from about eleven o'clock until early afternoon. Activity is often as brief as twenty minutes, and one should pick his fish in order to make time count. Fast rocky stretches produce the heaviest concentrations, and large fish can be found feeding where such water rushes into a pool or passes a deep backwater eddy.

This insect is of the clinging variety in its nymphal stage. Nymphs average about one-half inch in length and are typical of the genus *Epeorus*. Wing cases and the thorax are dark blackish brown. The abdomen and gills are a dark mottled brown. The legs and tails are a mottled brownish. Imitations are deadly fished dead-drift in the riffles. The Epeorus Nymph in sizes 10 and 12 is an excellent imitation.

Male Subimago or Dun
Tails—three-eighths inch, greyish

Body—three-eighths inch, brownish mottled back segments
  with rich maroon belly segments
Legs—greyish mottled with brown
Thorax—reddish brown
Eyes—large and dark
Wings—seven-sixteenths inch, dark bluish grey

Female Subimago or Dun

Tails—three-eighths inch, greyish
Body—seven-sixteenths inch, brownish mottled back segments
  with reddish brown belly segments
Legs—greyish mottled with brown
Thorax—reddish brown
Eyes—small and dark
Wings—one-half inch, dark bluish grey

As an imitation for both male and female duns I like the
Dark Red Quill in sizes 12 and 14. I have been unable thus
far to collect the imago flies and cannot find an instance of
their mating in several seasons of stream data. If an imitation
were needed, the Red Quill Spinner would probably serve
quite well.

The notes taken during this hatch on the Arkansas in 1948
emphasize an important rule of fishing: never assume an
insect's coloring without catching one first. I have seen this
done on widely scattered streams, and have been guilty of it
myself several times.

I was fishing the small meadow water above Leadville
Junction with a friend, and the preceding day's sport had been
excellent. The fish were not large on this pleasant little stream,
but they were numerous, and cagey enough to make the sport
intriguing. I had fished the pools carefully without results for
some time when a common mishap befell me. One moment I
was crossing a rocky riffle casually—and the next thing I knew
I was picking myself up off the bottom, thoroughly soaked.
The sensation of cold mountain water flowing just under one's
chin is chilling, but I survived to lay out my gear in the bright
high-altitude sunlight. I passed the next half hour watching

the still lifeless stream and the cumulus clouds that drifted over Mount Massive to the west. Then I turned to studying the nymph life in the riffle that had been my undoing and watching the raucous magpies nearby.

Finally my waders were dry again, and I put on my gear to start fishing. Dark clouds came from nowhere across the Mosquito peaks, and I was caught in a quiet, drizzling rain that barely disturbed the water. The stream came to life suddenly, and little May flies were everywhere on the water. Then the trout started to rise. I tried the Hendrickson that had worked so well on the preceding day, and was rewarded with a quick, splashy rise. I had missed seven fish before doubt arrived in my mind. Were these the same insects as before, or was my reflex on vacation? I missed another nice fish, and waded boldly into the pool to see what the flies really looked like. They were the maroon-bellied duns that were later identified as *Epeorus nitidus,* and were unknown to me at the time.

The next pool produced seven nice browns from ten to fourteen inches on the Dark Red Quill, and my reflex was thoroughly exonerated. Then the hatch was over as quickly as it began, and I returned to the car. My friend was waiting for me with an empty basket. He muttered something about my fly not working that day, and I told him that the hatch had changed. He had not bothered to examine the naturals at all. Too often I have done the same thing, only to play the fishless role in this narrative. Never match a hatch by looking at the flies in the air or on the water. Catch one or two and make sure.

Epeorus longimanus (Family Heptagenidae)

This little May fly is quite similar to its early-season relatives on Eastern streams. It has unusually long forelegs [also tails] in the male spinner, and this characteristic gives the *longimanus* species its name. Emergence and mating take place in late morning and early afternoon, and activity is confined to the swifter water.

Nymphs are typical of their genus and measure about three-eighths inch in length. The coloring is the dark mottled brown common in this group, and the thick, mottled legs are also found on the Eastern counterparts. The Epeorus Nymph is excellent in sizes 12 and 14. The naturals are clinging fast-water dwellers.

Male Subimago or Dun

Tails—three-eighths inch, mottled greyish
Body—three-eighths inch, greyish brown darkly ringed with brown
Legs—mottled greyish tan
Thorax—brownish
Eyes—large and dark
Wings—three-eighths inch, dark bluish grey

Female Subimago or Dun

Tails—seven-sixteenths inch, mottled greyish
Body—seven-sixteenths inch, greyish brown darkly ringed with brown
Legs—mottled greyish tan
Thorax—brownish
Eyes—large and dark
Wings—one-half inch, bluish grey

The Dark Gordon Quill tied in size 14 is an excellent male imitation. The Gordon Quill in size 12 imitates the female duns. The trout respond very well to this hatch, and it lasts for about one week.

Male Imago or Spinner

Tails—one and one-quarter inches, dark brownish
Body—three-eighths inch, reddish brown
Legs—mottled brownish
Thorax—brownish
Eyes—large and dark
Wings—three-eighths inch, glassy clear

Female Imago or Spinner

Tails—one and one-eighth inches, dark brownish

Body—seven-sixteenths inch, reddish brown with yellowish
    tan segments at the rear
Legs—mottled brown
Thorax—brownish
Eyes—small and dark
Wings—one-half inch, glassy clear

The males are imitated by a size 14 Red Quill Spinner, and
the Female Red Quill Spinner imitates the females in size 12.
The long forelegs of the male spinner often measure as much
as eleven-sixteenths inch. These spinner imitations are very
important flies on Western streams.

I once hit the Footbridge Pool of the Frying Pan at Ruedi
when the river was red hot. The trout were rising avidly to a
heavy spinner flight, and I took seven browns from thirteen to
eighteen inches. The fish came as fast as I could preen my fly
back into shape and make another cast. The whole once-in-a-
lifetime show was watched by a salmon-egging tourist who
had gone fishless on the bridge. I am quite sure he was con-
verted to the dry-fly technique. It is such a lucky episode as
this that cements one's reputation as an angler.

Ephemerella infrequens (Family Baetidae)

This little pale grey May fly is quite similar to the Eastern
flies of its genus, which make up the well-known Hendrickson
hatches. It emerges in the late morning on high-altitude
streams and is most common in the slower-moving stretches.
Hatches are not so concentrated as those of some of the other
Western species, but they are sufficiently important to warrant
the attention of anglers. The trout seem especially partial to
these May flies.

The nymphs are rather typical of the genus, being dark
greyish brown, paling to creamish grey on the undersides. The
tails are mottled greyish tan. The Dark Ephemerella Nymph
is an excellent imitative pattern.

There is nothing sporadic about emergence of this species;

it occurs at about eleven o'clock in the morning and lasts about a half hour. During the short hatching period the water is covered with duns, but the flies are present for only a few days.

Male Subimago or Dun

Tails—three-eighths inch, mottled grey
Body—three-eighths inch, greyish brown on the back segments
    paling to a creamish grey underneath
Legs—greyish tan
Thorax—greyish brown
Eyes—large and greyish
Wings—three-eighths inch, dark bluish grey

Female Subimago or Dun

Tails—seven-sixteenths inch, mottled greyish
Body—one-half inch, greyish brown on the back paling to a
    pinkish cream underneath
Legs—greyish tan
Thorax—greyish brown
Eyes—small and greyish
Wings—one-half inch, bluish grey

The Hendrickson dry fly in sizes 12 and 14 is an excellent imitation. This pattern has proved itself well on Western trout waters, and I have taken many large, selective fish with it.

Male Imago or Spinner

Tails—five-eighths inch, mottled tannish
Body—three-eighths inch, ruddy brown
Legs—greyish tan
Thorax—greyish brown
Eyes—large and dark
Wings—three-eighths inch, glassy clear

Female Imago or Spinner

Tails—one-half inch, mottled tannish
Body—one-half inch, greyish brown on the back with a
    yellowish cast underneath
Legs—yellowish grey
Thorax—greyish tan
Eyes—small and dark

Wings—one-half inch, glassy clear
Egg Sac—yellowish

The Little Rusty Spinner is a good imitation in size 14, and the Female Hendrickson with its little yellow ball of eggs is killing in size 12. The spinners mate about two days after they have emerged as duns. They drop their eggs from the air, but the brisk wind that seems to always be present in the mountains often blows many of them into the stream. The emergence and mating occur early in July on streams at around eight thousand feet.

Ephemerella grandis (Family Baetidae)

This large, juicy May fly is perhaps the most important insect of the season on many Western trout streams. It is on the water for about two weeks and is large enough to coax the really heavy fish to the surface. Emergence on high-altitude streams takes place in the late morning, while at around five thousand feet the hatching occurs just at twilight.

The nymphs are of the slow-water, clambering type, and are found in large numbers in the pools, runs and eddies of faster water. On the Gunnison in Colorado I once collected fifteen of them without moving from my seat on a flat rock at the edge of a large riffle. Naturals are about three-fourths inch in length. The wing cases and back segments are dirty greyish brown. The gills are greyish brown, as are the legs. The three tails are brown, with dark single marks on each tail. The belly segments are greyish, heavily banded with reddish brown. The naturals are quite juicy in appearance, and should be fished dead-drift. The Great Red Quill Nymph in size 10 is the imitation that I have used with much success. It produced a twenty-three-inch brown for me from a Colorado high lake.

Male Subimago or Dun
Tails—three-eighths inch, brownish with one dark brown mark on each tail

Body—one-half inch, greyish, deeply ringed with rich reddish
  brown
Legs—greyish tan mottled
Thorax—greyish tan mottled with brown
Eyes—large and dark
Wings—five-eighths inch, very bluish grey

Female Subimago or Dun

Tails—one-half inch, brownish with one dark brown mark on
  each tail
Body—five-eighths inch, greyish, deeply ringed with reddish
  brown
Legs—greyish tan mottled
Thorax—greyish tan mottled with brown
Eyes—small and dark
Wings—three-fourths inch, bluish grey

The Dark Great Red Quill imitates the male dun in a size
10. The Great Red Quill imitates the females in the same
size. These duns are present in the morning from about ten
o'clock until noon on streams above eight thousand feet in
elevation. At lower altitudes they emerge at about seven
o'clock in the evening. I have taken large fish in both morning
and evening on imitations of this hatch. On streams like the
Frying Pan, it is possible to take ten-pound limits in three or
four fish when these flies are hatching.

In my experience the spinner has never been too important
to the angler. Males and females are colored much as they
are in the dun stage, except that the imago wings are clear
and glassy, with faint traces of brown in the close veins of the
leading edges. The Great Red Quill Spinner is effective in
sizes 10 and 12 if the fish are found rising to the naturals.

Ephemerella grandis is extremely important to the angler and
as a trout food, for it is on the water at various altitudes from
early July until the middle of August. I have found specimens
emerging as late as September on some trout streams. By the
time it first appears, Western streams are at a fly-fishing peak.

WESTERN MAY FLIES: LATE SEASON

By the time summer has forced its way into the high country to bring out the tiny flowers of the timberline meadows and melt all but the permanent snow, the fly-fishing is at its seasonal peak. During the months of July and August the streams are dropping steadily, and the snow banks are gone from all but the highest ranges. These Western streams can never be called low or warm by Eastern late-summer standards, but they now are when compared to the June conditions.

As the season moves on into September, the nights become crisp and unpleasantly cold, even to a man in a sleeping bag. The purplish peaks acquire a fine mantle of new snow each night, which is gone by midday. By the middle of the month, the high country can be snowed in, and the aspens are rapidly turning to their rich golden yellow of autumn. The sky is unbelievably blue in this early fall, and the days are warm and invigorating, but there is ice in the water bucket each morning. Winter is just over the ridge.

Ephemerella inermis (Family Baetidae)

This pale little May fly is quite unlike anything on Eastern streams, for its coloring is a pale olive-yellow that is quite an elusive shade. It emerges in July on many streams, but I have found it in August on streams at high altitudes. My seasons on Western rivers found this hatch rather sparse, but angling friends tell me that it is often one of the best May fly hatches of the entire season on many streams.

Hatching takes place both in the morning and evening, with the scattered morning activity usually occuring between ten o'clock and one o'clock. Evening hatches start in the late afternoon, with the best activity coming around twilight. The nymphs are slow-water dwellers, and the best hatches are found on water of this type.

Nymphs measure about seven-sixteenths inch in length, with dark brownish grey wing cases and brownish grey thorax. The tails are tannish grey; the abdomen is greyish brown paling to a dirty tan on the undersides. The legs and eyes are greyish brown. The Ephemerella Nymph in sizes 12 and 14 is an excellent matching pattern.

Male Subimago or Dun
Tails—three-eighths inch, tannish
Body—three-eighths inch, tannish
Legs—tannish
Thorax—tannish grey
Eyes—large and greyish
Wings—three-eighths inch, pale olive-yellow

Female Subimago or Dun
Tails—seven-sixteenths inch, tannish
Body—seven-sixteenths inch, tannish
Legs—tannish
Thorax—tannish grey
Eyes—small and greyish
Wings—one-half inch, pale olive-yellow

The imitative pattern was developed by Frank Klune and myself on the Frying Pan in 1948. It was most effective in sizes 12 and 14, and was later christened the Pale Olive Quill, after a seventeen-inch brown had fallen to it on the glassy Ruedi

Stillwater. The selective feeders of that pool were our criteria of success.

According to friends who frequent the Colorado rivers during this hatch, imitation of these duns was quite an enigma for many seasons. All of the commerical olive flies were too dark or too greenish for success. Pale ginger flies produced a few gullible fish, but rarely anything over fifteen inches fell to them. Finally I located a dyed pale olive-grey neck that looked good. On the first evening that we fished the dry flies from this neck, the members of our party accounted for two ten-pound limits in nine fish. The browns were too selective to be easily fooled.

This selectivity seems to be rather acute during the emergence of *Ephemerella inermis*. Frank Klune described it in a letter some seasons ago in which he wrote: "During the Pale Olive hatches the trout become extremely choosy, especially in beaver ponds and still pools. Very slight differences in the color of the artificial may mean the difference between catching a large number of big trout or none at all. The fish seem to be fooled more easily on dark days than on bright ones with the olive flies. My theory is this: sunlight affects these olive hackles in an unusual way making the artificial appear quite unlike the dull-colored pale olive naturals." Although it does contradict the sunlight-and-shadow theorems, this seems to be true with respect to this particular hackle.

I have never witnessed a spinner flight of this species, and would presume their mating is unimportant to the trout fisherman. Perhaps on some stream in the future I will collect the naturals and fish an imitation.

Epeorus albertae (Family Heptagenidae)

This diminutive May fly is one of the most important Western hatches in spite of its size. It is similar to several Eastern hatches, except in its spinner stages. I have taken fish up to three pounds on the imitations of this species. It emerges in

July and early August on streams around five to six thousand feet in elevation. Hatching occurs at twilight.

Nymphs measure about one-quarter inch in length and are a dirty greyish tan. They are found primarily in the faster stretches of the riffles and white water. Since the adult duns emerge under water in the manner of their genus, the tiny Pink Lady wet fly is a better imitation than the Epeorus Nymph. The nymph seems to be effective in size 16 before hatching commences. The wet-fly imitation in the same size is better after the actual emergence is under way.

I first became aware of the effectiveness of a wet-fly imitation when my sunken dry fly took a brace of two-pounders from a tiny pocket on the Frying Pan. The evening before I had floated a dry fly over that same spot during the height of the hatch without results. The resulting experiments with wet flies produced larger trout than I had been able to take during this hatch before. The purist can have his fun with trout up to seventeen inches, which was my best on the dry fly, but for the really large fish rising during this hatch he will have to fish the sunken fly.

Male Subimago or Dun

Tails—one-quarter inch, cream
Body—one-quarter inch, creamish faintly marked with brown on the back, elusive pink cast to the sternites
Legs—mottled cream
Thorax—creamish tan
Eyes—large and greyish
Wings—one-quarter inch, greyish

Female Subimago or Dun

Tails—five-sixteenths inch, cream
Body—three-eighths inch, creamish marked with brown on the back, pinkish cast underneath
Legs—cream
Thorax—creamish tan
Eyes—small and greyish
Wings—three-eighths inch, greyish

My favorite dry-fly imitation for both males and females is a modified Pink Lady dressing in sizes 16 and 18. It has proved to be most effective on the most critical brown trout of the Pan.

Male Imago or Spinner

Tails—one inch, dark mottled grey
Body—five-sixteenths inch, creamish grey ringed with delicate brown markings, last two segments brownish
Legs—greyish mottled
Thorax—greyish brown
Eyes—large and greyish
Wings—five-sixteenths inch, glassy clear

Female Imago or Spinner

Tails—three-quarters inch, light brownish
Body—three-eighths inch, light brownish marked with brown on the back segments, slight pinkish cast
Legs—light brownish
Thorax—light brownish
Eyes—small and grey
Wings—three-eighths inch, glassy clear

The Male Salmon Spinner imitates the males in size 18, while the Little Salmon Spinner is an excellent female imitation in size 16. The mating takes place over the riffles at twilight, and I have had some excellent fishing with imitative patterns.

Heptagenia elegantula (Family Heptagenidae)

This dark little May fly has been rather important in the dun stage, but as yet I have not been able to secure nymphs or spinners of the species. It is a morning hatch, which appears at around eleven o'clock and lasts for about forty-five minutes. There are usually large numbers of these flies present during this activity.

Male Subimago or Dun

Tails—five-sixteenths inch, dark greyish

Body—five-sixteenths inch, dark greyish heavily banded with
very rich brown
Legs—brownish grey
Thorax—brownish
Eyes—large and dark
Wings—three-eighths inch, dark bluish grey

Female Subimago or Dun
Tails—three-eighths inch, greyish
Body—seven-sixteenths inch, greyish ringed with dark brown
at the segments
Legs—brownish grey
Thorax—brownish
Eyes—small and greyish
Wings—seven-sixteenths inch, dark bluish grey

The familiar Dark Gordon Quill in sizes 12 and 14 is a good imitation. Notes recall one particular morning when this hatch was important. I was on the Taylor in Colorado when these little duns started coming off the riffles in large numbers. It was about ten minutes after eleven o'clock. For several more minutes there was not a rise to be seen up and down the river. Then, as if by some signal, there were rises everywhere. There was no drag problem on the swift thigh-deep run that I was working, and the fishing was almost too easy. Seventy-five yards of water gave up twenty-nine fish of between ten and seventeen inches. Then the hatch was over abruptly. I waded to the car contented, with the three largest fish in my basket. Such fishing is exciting and good for the confidence, but it is rarely as much fun as fishing a selective fish in some difficult current or brush-protected spot.

Paraleptophlebia packii (Family Baetidae)

This diminutive species is fairly common on Western trout waters. It is of the slow-water type, and the best hatches come from the pools. Trout are eager to feed upon this hatch, and it affords the angler a chance for some good light-tackle dry-fly sport. Hatching generally begins in late morning and lasts sporadically for much of the day.

Western anglers find these May flies just as perplexing as Eastern anglers who must cope with others of their size. The fish will not take imitations larger than about size 16, and smaller sizes are better. Many trout fishermen regard such flies as mere playthings, for men interested in light tackle for small fish. Nothing could be more distant from the truth. My best fish on a size 20 fly went twenty inches, and I have lost larger ones.

The nymph of this species measures about one-quarter inch in length, and its general coloring is greyish brown. The wing cases are rather dark. This particular nymph seems to be appealing to the trout, and I have had some fine sport fishing its imitations to actual rises. The Leptophlebia Nymph in size 16 is a good pattern for this.

Male Subimago or Dun

Tails—one-quarter inch, greyish
Body—one-quarter inch, greyish
Legs—greyish
Thorax—greyish
Eyes—olive-greyish
Wings—one-quarter inch, dark bluish grey

Female Subimago or Dun

Tails—one-quarter inch, greyish
Body—five-sixteenths inch, greyish with an olive cast
Legs—greyish
Thorax—greyish
Eyes—olive-greyish
Wings—three-eighths inch, dark bluish grey

The Dark Blue Quill is an excellent imitation of the males in size 18. The Iron Blue Dun in size 16 is a good female pattern. It is fascinating to watch these tiny dry flies bob along some grassy undercut bank or down some narrow channel in the weeds and disappear in a healthy swirl.

Female Imago or Spinner

Tails—three-eighths inch, greyish white
Body—five-sixteenths inch, greyish ringed

Legs—greyish
Thorax—greyish
Eyes—small and dark
Wings—three-eighths inch, glassy clear

These little spinners appear four days after the duns have hatched. The males are colored exactly like the females; the male tails measure about seven-sixteenths inch. The Blue Quill Spinner is good, in size 16 and smaller.

I cannot help but relate one incident that occured during one of these *Paraleptophlebia* hatches on a river that we shall leave nameless. I was host to three beginners. The little flies had been emerging in good numbers for two days, and I expected another good hatch at about ten o'clock. My neophyte friends were skeptical when I told them we would start fishing at ten. They were oriented to the get-up-at-dawn school of fishing thought. At ten o'clock we left our cabin and started to the river, a distance of about two hundred feet. My friends refused to bring their rods, preferring to watch and ask questions. One of the three was a sharp fellow who not only asked what I was doing, but also why it was being done. With that inquisitive approach, it is doubtful that he remained in the ranks of the beginners for very long.

We selected a large flat pool for the classroom, where there was a gravel bar well situated for the students. The little duns appeared right on time, and it was not long before several good fish were working. The session was broken up by a hard rain that started after a half hour, but I was able to take three fish between twelve and nineteen inches on my little Iron Blue Dun. My friends were extremely excited over these fish, for their largest had been a ten-inch rainbow on a wet fly in rough water. They refused to believe that the three fish were unusual, in spite of my statements to the contrary. I could probably not again take three fish like that in front of an audience in the next million years.

Callibaetis pallidus (Family Baetidae)

Except for the fact that it is slightly smaller and has only two tails in the adult, this pale May fly is identical to the pale olive species earlier treated. These smaller pale olives are present in late August on quiet streams and beaver ponds. Lazy meadow streams with good weed growths in their quiet stretches are a perfect habitat.

The nymph is about five-sixteenths inch in length, with greyish wing cases, long mottled legs, a greyish cream abdomen with darker brownish mottlings, and three greyish tails with brownish markings near the tips. It has an elusive greenish cast. The Callibaetis Nymph in sizes 14 and 16 is a good imitation. This little nymph is very agile in the water, and the artificial should be fished with a slow, darting retrieve.

Male Subimago or Dun
Tails—one-quarter inch, creamish
Body—five-sixteenths inch, creamish tan
Legs—tannish
Thorax—tannish
Eyes—greyish
Wings—five-sixteenths inch, pale olive-yellow

Female Subimago or Dun
Tails—one-quarter inch, creamish
Body—three-eighths inch, creamish tan
Legs—tannish
Thorax—tannish
Eyes—greyish
Wings—seven-sixteenths inch, pale olive-yellow

These duns are well represented by the Pale Olive Quill in sizes 14 and 16. The spinner stage acquires glassy wings in the final moulting, and the tails of the male lengthen by about one-eighth inch. The Ginger Quill Spinner in sizes 14 and 16 imitates it quite well. It is not too important to the angler.

Stenonema verticus (Family Heptagenidae)

This pale cream May fly is quite similar to the Eastern hatches of its genus. It is well distributed in Western waters, and emerges in late afternoon and evening. The famous Gunnison in Colorado has hatches in August. I have seen these flies on the water by the hundreds.

The nymphs are about five-sixteenths inch in length, with greyish wing cases, dirty greyish bodies and gills, greyish mottled legs and three speckled tails. They are fast-water dwellers. The Stenonema Nymph in sizes 14 and 16 is an excellent imitation. It should be fished dead-drift in the riffles.

Male Subimago or Dun

Tails—three-sixteenths inch, creamish
Body—one-quarter inch, creamish lightly marked with brown on the back segments
Legs—cream, lightly banded on each femur
Thorax—cream
Eyes—large and dark
Wings—five-sixteenths inch, cream with slightly darker markings in the veins of greyish brown

Female Subimago or Dun

Tails—one-quarter inch, creamish
Body—three-eighths inch, creamish lightly marked with brown on the back segments
Legs—cream, lightly banded on each femur
Thorax—cream
Eyes—small and dark
Wings—seven-sixteenths inch, cream with light brownish vein markings

The Eastern Paulinskill dry-fly pattern is an imitation in sizes 14 and 16. It has produced well on Western streams during these hatches. The duns moult into an imago stage with glassy clear wings and body rather tannish in color. The tails of the male extend to about three-eighths inch. The Ginger Quill Spinner in sizes 14 and 16 will take fish when an imitation is needed.

One of the sorriest displays of technique I have ever seen occurred during this hatch. The characters in the tragic drama were myself and one fifteen-inch brown trout. This particular fish was rising freely along a log jam in a side channel of the Gunnison, and he took my Paulinskill on the first float. I am sorry that I ever hooked him. He raced quickly across the little pool and leaped over a snag, coming down in a brush-filled eddy. I waded quickly across the waist-deep stream and disengaged him somehow before he could break off. With complete ingratitude he squirted between my legs and threshed wildly behind me on the surface. He was still on when that dilemma was remedied, and went promptly back into the brush. I succeeded in untangling things a second time, falling in clumsily in the process and ruining an allegedly waterproof watch. Bedlam continued for several more minutes. I released the fish with relief and respect, glad that I was completely alone.

Callibaetis americanus (Family Baetidae)

This little greyish mottled May fly is quite important on slow weedy water, which is conducive to their species. It is rather common on lakes and beaver ponds, and since the genus is many-brooded, there are two main hatching periods each season. The first activity takes place in July, and the second emergence occurs late in August. My principle experience with the hatch has been on high lakes at around nine thousand feet.

The nymphs are active in the water and clamber about through the weeds with great agility. They average about five-sixteenths to three-eighths inch in length. The legs are long and delicate, with dark markings at the joints. The wing cases and bodies are greyish brown. The gills are mottled brown. The three tails are marked with brown near the tips. The sternites are an olive-greyish. The Callibaetis Nymph is deadly in size 16 when fished with a very slow twitching retrieve.

Male Subimago or Dun

Tails—three-sixteenths inch, greyish
Body—one-quarter inch, greyish ringed
Legs—greyish, marked at the joints
Thorax—greyish
Eyes—large and dark grey
Wings—one-quarter inch, grey heavily mottled in black

Female Subimago or Dun

Tails—one-quarter inch, greyish
Body—three-eighths inch, greyish ringed
Legs—greyish, marked at the joints
Thorax—greyish
Eyes—small and greyish
Wings—three-eighths inch, grey and mottled

These May flies hatch in the afternoon and are often on the water by the hundreds. On Granite Lake in Colorado I have seen them drifting with the wind riffles until the downwind side of the water was covered with them. The browns and Kamloops rainbows wasted little time. My favorite imitation is the Grey Quill in size 16.

Male Imago or Spinner

Tails—one-half inch, greyish

PLATE THREE: MAY FLIES *(opposite)*

Ephemerella grandis male dun; *Ephemerella grandis* female dun; *Ephemerella inermis* male dun; *Ephemerella inermis* female dun; *Epeorus albertae* male dun.

Epeorus albertae female dun; *Heptagenia elegantula* male dun; *Heptagenia elegantula* female dun; *Paraleptophlebia packii* male dun; *Paraleptophlebia packii* female dun.

Callibaetis pallidus male dun; *Callibaetis pallidus* female dun; *Stenonema verticus* male dun; *Stenonema verticus* female dun; *Callibaetis americanus* male dun.

Callibaetis americanus female dun; *Siphlonurus occidentalis* male dun; *Siphlonurus occidentalis* female dun; *Baetis* sp. female dun; *Baetis* sp. male dun.

Epeorus pleuralis male spinner; *Epeorus pleuralis* female spinner; *Paraleptophlebia adoptiva* male spinner; *Epeorus vitrea* female spinner; *Ephemerella dorothea* male spinner.

Ephemerella subvaria male spinner; *Ephemerella subvaria* female spinner; *Leptophlebia cupida* male spinner; *Leptophlebia cupida* female spinner; *Ephemerella dorothea* female spinner.

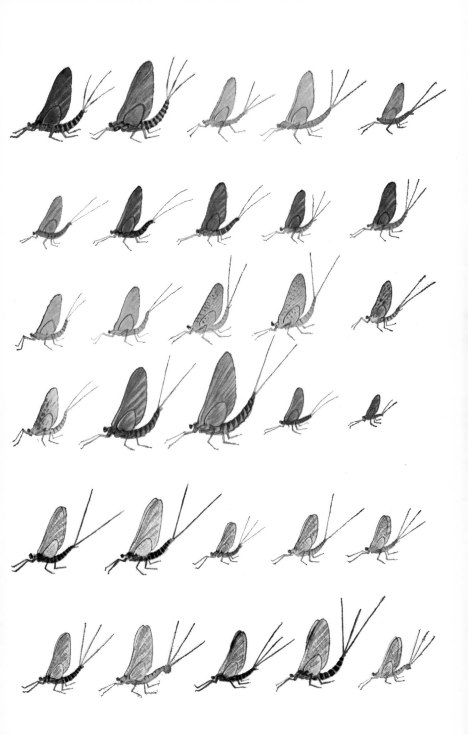

Body—one-quarter inch, greyish ringed
Legs—greyish, marked at the joints
Thorax—greyish
Eyes—large and greyish
Wings—one-quarter inch, glassy clear flecked with dark grey
   along the leading edges

Female Imago or Spinner

Tails—seven-sixteenths inch, greyish
Body—three-eighths inch, greyish ringed
Legs—greyish, marked at the joints
Thorax—greyish
Eyes—small and greyish
Wings—three-eighths inch, glassy clear lightly mottled with
   greyish brown

The Grey Quill Spinner is an excellent imitative pattern in
size 16. I have used it with great success on Western trout waters.

Siphlonurus occidentalis (Family Baetidae)

This large bluish grey May fly hatches on Western trout
waters in August and September. Hatching is quite sporadic
and usually occurs during the daylight hours. The Eastern
species of this genus are important as spinners, but I have not
yet witnessed a major spinner flight on our Western streams.

The nymph is of the swimming type and frequents the
slower streams and beaver ponds. It measures about three-
quarters inch in length. The wing cases are dark brownish
grey, the thorax and abdomen greyish, the tannish grey legs
are marked with brown, the gills are flat and brownish, and
the three brownish tails are marked with darker brown. The
Siphlonurus Nymph in sizes 10 and 12 is a fine fly. The
nymphs are quite agile in the water, darting about like tiny
minnows. Their tantalizing behavior and fairly large size make
them very attractive to the trout. Artificials should be fished
with an action suggestive of the swimming habits of the naturals.

Male Subimago or Dun

Tails—one-quarter inch, greyish

Body—one-half inch, greyish marked with brown
Legs—greyish marked with brown
Thorax—grey mottled with brown
Eyes—large and dark greyish
Wings—five-eighths inch, very dark blue-grey

Female Subimago or Dun
Tails—one-half inch, greyish
Body—five-eighths inch, greyish ringed with brown
Legs—greyish marked with brown
Thorax—greyish mottled with brown
Eyes—small and greyish
Wings—three-quarters inch, bluish grey

The large cutthroats and rainbows of the Yellowstone feed avidly on this hatch in September, and I have raised some veritable monsters to imitations. The Dark Grey Drake in size 10 imitates the males, and the Light Grey Drake in size 8 represents the females. Both patterns are variations of the popular Eastern Grey Wulff dressing.

Genus Baetis (Family Baetidae)

The little May flies of the genus *Baetis* are very important to the Western angler, for they are common on those waters. They emerge during the day, with hatching scattered from ten o'clock in the morning until about four o'clock in the afternoon. These flies are generally greyish blue in coloring, with abdomens running from dull greyish to a dirty olive-yellow. They measure about three-eighths inch in the wings and bodies, and some hatches are even smaller.

The nymphs are the darkly mottled brownish naturals characteristic of their genus. They have been described as rather fishlike in shape. The average nymph seems to measure from one-quarter to three-eighths inch in length. As a representation, the Baetis Nymph works well in a 16.

To imitate the various duns of this prolific genus I tie three dry flies in sizes 16 through 22. The Blue Quill is familiar to all anglers and needs no introduction here. I have found it most effective in late August on the streams that lie at around nine thousand feet. The venerable Iron Blue Dun is another that works well, especially in the smaller sizes, and I have had my best luck with it on the Firehole in the Yellowstone country during late September. On the Gunnison and other streams at around five thousand feet I have used the little Blue-winged Olive Dun with good results in August. Since these *Baetis* flies are many-brooded, one can expect to find them all season at varying altitudes.

According to Dr. Ann Haven Morgan, the spinners of this genus go under water to oviposit. The female leaves the mating swarm to find a suitable spot, usually going under water on a rock, log, plant stem or bridge abutment. In moving through the surface film she folds her wings about her abdomen and uses the downstream side of the object she has selected. The passing through the surface film is the critical phase of her mating. When she is once under the surface, she inspects the rock or log carefully with her abdomen. Finally she lays her eggs with a circular sweeping motion, which leaves a little row of eggs each time. When her supply of eggs is exhausted she climbs back out of the water or is swept away in the underwater currents.

This underwater egg-laying makes wet flies suggestive of the *Baetis* excellent during the mating activity. Two patterns that have been mentioned before, the Ginger Quill Spinner and the Blue Quill Spinner, are deadly in sizes 16 and 18. Dry-fly versions are also useful.

The diminutive size of these May flies often leads anglers to consider them of little importance. No greater mistake could be made. My stream notes are filled with days that were successful because of this species. One morning on the Biscuit Basin stretch of the Firehole I moved forty-two trout of some ten to eighteen inches. They were all raised on the Iron Blue Dun and none were retained. The hook of my imitation was size 20.

CADDIS FLIES AND STONE FLIES

THE CADDIS FLIES are fairly important to both Eastern and Western anglers, particularly when there are no May flies present. The stone flies are not too significant to Eastern fishermen except on rocky mountain streams, but the swift Western rivers find them extremely important as trout food. The large stone fly hatches found on Western streams are not duplicated in the Eastern waters.

We have learned that the caddis flies constitute the order Trichoptera and the stone flies make up the order Plecoptera. Many Eastern and Western species are quite similar, and the same artificials work for both natural flies.

Since these insect orders are not often found in concentrated numbers, we will not attempt to discuss their myriad species as individual hatches. Imitation of the various genera is sufficient for the purposes of the angler. The caddis flies are more numerous than the stone flies, numbering over nine hundred species indigenous to our waters. When one sees how many species there are, he can realize how pointless it would be to classify and imitate each natural insect. Some of the individual species typical of their genera have been described, but in view of the numerous forms that emerge from our streams it is best that specific insects be treated generally. This is a practical approach.

Caddis Flies (Order Trichoptera)

The many caddis fly genera common on our trout waters each have individualistic larval cases by which they may be identified by the angler. The genus *Arctoecia* builds its cases of leaf fragments, forming them into a structure that measures about one-half inch in length and is triangular in cross section. The genus *Brachycentrus* puts wood and plant fibers together into tapered cases that are rectangular in section and measure from one-quarter to one-half inch in length. Adult flies of *Arctoecia* average about one-half inch in length. Their wings are mottled cinnamon brown, the legs are reddish grey, and the abdomens are yellowish brown. The rear wings are a sandy yellow, but they are exposed to the view of the trout only when the caddis flies are in flight above the water. The Cinnamon Sedge is a good imitation of the *Arctoecia* flies in sizes 12 and 14. The *Brachycentrus* genus includes the insects commonly known to anglers as the Grannom hatches. These flies have mottled brownish wings, greyish legs, greyish brown bodies that are darkly ringed; and the females carry greenish yellow egg sacs at the rear of their abdomens. They are common on Eastern trout streams in early season, the species being *Brachycentrus fuliginosus*. The Male Grannom is an excellent imitation of this genus in sizes 12 and 14. The Female Grannom imitates the egg-filled females in the same sizes. This genus can assume the importance of a hatch.

The little *Chimarra* flies are net-spinners in the larval stage, and do not build protective cases. They fashion weblike nets between rocks in the stream bed, and catch their food from the current with them. The adults are rather small, averaging about one-third inch in length. They are a dark blackish grey in coloring. The Little Black Caddis is an excellent fly in size 16.

The genus *Psilotreta* is rather important to anglers on many waters. The larvae build cornucopia-like cases, of sand and tiny pebbles, that average about one-half inch in length. The adult flies of this genus are generally known to the fisherman as Dark Blue Sedges. The wings are dark bluish grey, the legs are brownish grey, and the bodies are brownish ringed with dark grey. The antennae are a dirty yellow. The Dark Blue Sedge is an excellent imitation of these fast-water caddis flies in sizes 12 and 14.

The net-spinning genera *Arctopsyche* and *Hydropsyche* are common on our trout streams. They average about one-third inch in length. The wings are a mottled brownish grey, the legs are greyish, and the bodies are greyish with slightly darker ringing. The Dark Caddis Quill is an excellent imitation in sizes 14 and 16. This is an unusually good general imitation of the Trichoptera, and the story of its orgin is told in a later chapter.

The species of the genus *Rhyacophila* range about freely in the larval stages. They are fast-water dwellers, and are known as Green and Brown Caddis Flies to the angler. The Brown Sedge is a fine imitation in sizes 12 and 14. The Green Sedge works well as an imitation of the greenish species. The larvae are greenish white and average about five-eighths inch in length.

The genera *Stenophylax* and *Platyphylax* build their stick cases of bits of bark and wood. They are quiet-water dwellers and are nocturnal in emergence. Hatching takes place on warm nights, and the big flies are common over the water after dark. Big trout will often night-feed on these juicy naturals. The adults are generally a medium mottled brownish in coloring. They are particularly common on Eastern waters in late summer, and good night fishing can be enjoyed with the Dark Brown Sedge in sizes 6 through 10. The larvae and adults average about three-quarters to one inch in length.

The genus *Limnophilus* forms thick tubular cases of stones and sand. It is common in ponds and the slower streams. The turtle-like gravel huts of the genus *Glossosoma* are common in fast water. The *Macronemum* larvae are net-spinners of swift water.

These various larval types are imitated by several patterns suggestive of the more common genera. The Psilotreta Larva, Green Caddis Larva, Caddis Worm, Stick Caddis and Cased Caddis are all excellent. Sizes 8 through 14 are useful to the angler.

Caddis Pupa and Larva

The pupal stage becomes very important in species that emerge in large numbers at a given time. Then the pupae are migrating to the surface. The Green Caddis Pupa, Dark Caddis Pupa and Light Caddis Pupa are three good patterns in sizes 8 to 14.

The general adult imitations recommended are effective fished wet or dry. They are often deadly when twitched gently across the surface at twilight. As much line as possible should be kept off the water when this skating technique is used. Many species dip into the water to oviposit, and often run across the surface. Perhaps the twilight skating is suggestive of this trait. Rises to the flies worked in this manner are usually rather splashy and sudden. I first learned this system from a German angler who used it to take the large cannibal browns out of his water on the pleasant Wiesandt. It is deadly.

Occasionally it is valuable to have dry flies suggestive of the Trichoptera in flight. There are several so-called fancy patterns that are very successful on selective fish. I think they owe their results to the simulation of a flying caddis. Two of the best are the well-known Adams and the rather recent Whitcraft. The Adams came from the prolific vise of old Len Halladay of Mayfield, Michigan, and was first fished on the Boardman by Charles Adams. The Whitcraft is a product of Don Martinez and was born in the Yellowstone country of the Wyoming-Idaho-Montana corner. These two flies are excellent in sizes 10 through 16.

These general larval, pupal and adult caddis fly imitations should serve the angler well. The order is so large that a new species is always a possibility.

Stone Flies (Order Plecoptera)

Although they form a minor portion of the trout diet in Eastern waters, the stone flies become rather important on swift Western streams. They are of great value on those rivers that have the heavy hatches of large stone flies known as salmon or willow flies.

The stone fly season is begun in both East and West by the tiny dark genus *Capnia*. These insects measure about three-eighths inch in length, and their nymphs are imitated by the Early Brown Stone Fly Nymph in sizes 14 and 16. The Little Black Stone Fly imitates the adults in sizes 14 and 16. These insects are often called snow flies, and good fishing may be experienced with imitations if the water is clear.

Capnia Adult

Other early genera are *Taeniopteryx* and *Strophopteryx*. They vary from blackish to brownish in both the nymph and adult, and measure about one-half inch in length. The nymphs are imitated by the Early Brown Stone Fly Nymph in sizes 14 and 16. Adults are well represented in the same sizes by the Little Black Stone Fly of Charles Wetzel and the Early Brown Stone Fly of Theodore Gordon. I have had some excellent fishing when these flies were present.

The large flies of the genus *Acroneuria* are of importance in both East and West, although the nymphal stage is the more important on Eastern streams. There are many species of this genus on our waters. The nymphs are known as hellgrammites in the Western regions, and as water crickets on some Eastern streams. The excellent Stone Fly Nymph created by my good friend and tutor, Bill Blades, is a first-rate imitation in sizes 8 and 10. The adults are imitated by the Willow Fly, a modification of a local Western pattern by that name. It is best fished in sizes 8 and 10. The species *Acroneuria pacifica* makes up part of the famous willow fly hatches on Western rivers. These heavy mating flights occur on the Gunnison in late June, and are really a spectacle to see. The naturals are gulped by fish up to ten pounds in weight, and are often used as bait for dapping work with deadly effect.

The important genus *Perla* is well represented on our trout streams. The adults are known simply as stone flies on Eastern waters. On Western streams they are included in the willow fly–salmon fly excitement. The nymphs are the large amber-mottled and banded species common in our waters. The Blades Stone Fly recommended for the *Acroneuria* nymph is good in sizes 6 and 8. The Stone Fly pattern recommended by Wetzel in *Practical Fly Fishing* is an excellent Eastern fly in sizes 8 and 10. The slightly larger Hair Stone Fly is a good Western imitation in sizes 6 and 8.

Taeniopteryx Nymph

The large *Pteronarcys* flies are found on both the Eastern and Western streams. They are nocturnal in the East, and are of only occasional importance to night fishermen, but on Western rivers they make up most of the salmon fly hatch. The nymphs and adults are generally over one inch in length. On some waters these flies are much larger, and make a mouthful for the largest trout. The nymphs are the common blackish brown species found under the stones in the riffles. They too are known as hellgrammites to Western anglers, and are used in large numbers as live bait. The use of these nymphs for bait is seriously upsetting the natural balance of food in the rivers. One wonders if the naturals can stand the toll taken by both man and natural enemies. This criticism may be read to a chorus of laughter by Western anglers, because there are still so many of the nymphs. But they are fewer each season, and the blizzard-like flights may dwindle into flurries. Other skeptics in other years thought the buffalo countless.

Several patterns have been developed to imitate these big stone fly adults. On Eastern trout streams the Giant Stone Fly created by Ed Sens has seen excellent service as a night-fishing wet fly. It is tied in size 6. It is best in the pools after dark in July and August. For the Western activity I have used the Western Salmon Fly with very good results. It is dressed in sizes 4 and 6.

Adults of the genus *Leuctra* are called needle flies because they roll their wings to a point. They are not too numerous in my experience, but trout seem to relish them for some reason. They are a dark brownish grey and measure about seven-sixteenths inch in length. I like the Mallard Quill wet fly in size 16 as an imitation. The wing should be rolled and sparse, with a little lacquer to point the tip.

The pale little flies of the genus *Alloperla* are common on Eastern and Western rivers. The nymphs are a dirty yellowish grey and measure about seven-sixteenths inch. The adult flies are about the same size, and have greyish bodies with a greenish yellow cast and greyish wings. The nymphs are imitated by the Yellow Stone Fly Nymph in size 14. The Little Green Stone Fly in size 14 represents the adults.

The genus *Isoperla* is another common group of pale stone flies found on our waters. The nymphs are greyish tan and measure about one-half inch in length. The adults are known as Yellow Sallies by many fishermen. The nymphs are imitated by the Yellow Stone Fly Nymph in sizes 12 and 14. The Little Yellow Stone Fly seems to work well when the adults are present. It should be tied in sizes 12 and 14.

All of these stone fly patterns are effective fished wet or dry. It is advisable to keep the tying flexible in all insect imitations. This has been practiced for some time by many fly tiers. In the smaller sizes the wets can be dressed with down-wings tied flat over the body and a conventional wet-fly beard hackling. The smaller dry-fly versions can be tied in much the same manner and then hackled like a regular dry fly. Then the flat down-wings are added. The dressing is completed by trimming off the hackle fibers on the top and bottom, creating a dry fly that rides flat in the surface film like the naturals. This style of tying stone fly imitations was developed by Edward Ringwood Hewitt for his famous Neversink flats.

The larger wet flies can be dressed in a conventional manner and then finished with bent trimmed-hackle legs in place of the hackles. These are best for selective fish in quite water. In the big brawling white-water stretches, a big fully-hackled fly with hair wings is deadly. The hair stone flies are a product of Western rivers, and primarily of the fly vise of Don Harger in Oregon. Lee Wulff has also come up with some hair stone flies on the Battenkill in the New York–Vermont area.

The fly tier must be versatile enough to adapt his creations to the demands of different water types. There are many conditions requiring variations in dressing. Since the most exacting water is quiet and glassy, the patterns recommended here and elsewhere in the book have been devised and developed for its limitations.

THE LESSER TROUT FOODS

ANGLERS ARE all too familiar with the hatches that cause selectivity, but there are times when they may find the trout feeding upon the lesser foods. Fish are not often selective when feeding upon these minor forms, but one must always be prepared for that possibility. There are both aquatic and non-aquatic forms that are being placed in this less-important category.

Perhaps the terrestrial insects most commonly known to the angler are the grasshoppers, ants and beetles. Small crustacea also find their way into the trout diet. Crane flies, alder flies, damsel flies, dragonflies, back swimmers, beetles and midges are all aquatic lesser foods. Imitations of these insects may be carried in what Al McClane of *Field & Stream* has aptly called the "odd box." In it are carried those flies that are not often needed in fishing.

Trout are not often selective to these minor foods because one rarely finds them in concentrated numbers. Midges, flying ants and alder flies are exceptions.

The order Diptera makes up a very large part of the lesser foods taken by the trout. The insects of this order have two wings and a pair of rear wings that are atrophied into little clublike appendages called halteres. The Diptera are known as the two-winged flies. The order has a complete life cycle consisting of egg, larva, pupa and adult. The Diptera are one of the largest insect orders, numbering over sixteen thousand North American species. About one-fifth of these are of an aquatic nature. Of the numerous families and genera, only the crane flies and midges are of real importance to fishermen.

Crane flies are members of the family Tipulidae and are the largest of the two-winged flies taken by trout. They are the large mosquito-like insects commonly seen by all of us on summer nights. They are quite numerous along the stream, clinging to the stones and foliage with their long delicate legs. They rarely hatch in any real quantity, and are important only when nothing better is on the water.

Crane Fly Larva

The larvae are wormlike, and measure from about one-half inch to two inches in length depending upon species. They live both in the water and in the moist earth of banks and lowlands. Known to anglers as water worms, these larvae are sometimes fed upon eagerly by the trout. Their exact habits vary with species. The larval stage lasts about one year. The little larvae are semi-transparent, and their coloring runs from creamish to light brown. They are principally vegetarian.

The pupal stage lasts approximately one to three weeks depending upon species. It is usually spent out of the water in a pupal burrow. Species that pupate in the water are of some interest to the angler. The adult fly usually emerges in late morning. By flexing its body the crane fly splits the pupal skin and crawls out. If the pupal period is spent out of the water, it waddles clumsily away, leaving its pupal skin in the burrow. If the pupa is aquatic, its emergence is much like that of other orders.

Adult crane flies do not feed to any great extent, but the nectar of plants and blossoms is a source of nutrition. Because they eat after leaving the water, the crane flies are often present for some time.

Windy weather often blows large numbers of crane flies into the stream from bankside resting places. In the Western mountains, where wind is ever present, the crane flies are sometimes important to the fisherman. Another time when they assume some importance is during mating. They are rather clumsy in flight, and are extremely so when joined in copula. They often fall into the water together and are taken by the trout.

Crane Fly Pupa

The largest of the crane fly genera is the *Tipula* group, which is well distributed throughout our trout waters. It includes some of the largest species, which measure as much as two inches in the bodies. Such naturals are almost too large for good imitation. Important Eastern species are *Tipula bicornis* and *Tipula furca*. In Western areas the genus is represented by flies like *Tipula dorsimacula*. The species *furca* is well known to anglers, with its heavily streaked wings, greenish olive abdomen, brownish thorax and long olive-brown legs. It is known as the Whirling Crane Fly.

Tipula pendulifera is a common Western species with glassy wings, an orangish brown body with dark bands of brown, a brownish thorax and long brownish legs. It is familiar to Western anglers in August.

The Little Yellow Crane Flies are found in fast water and belong to the genus *Antocha*. They are fairly common, and have glassy whitish wings, creamish yellow thorax, tannish yellow abdomen and long pale ginger legs. These little flies seem to love damp rainy weather.

These species are fairly representative of the crane flies as a family. Imitation of the thousands of species is impractical, and the angler must rely on artificials that suggest the group as a whole.

Larval imitations should be fished dead-drift near the bottom, and a little fuse wire wrapped under the body of the artificials will help. Three excellent patterns are the Green

Crane Fly Larva, Brown Crane Fly Larva and White Crane Fly Larva. They should be dressed in sizes 8 through 14. They are most commonly found in the trout diet during the run-off after the streams have been high and roily.

Crane Fly

Pupal imitations should be fished twitchingly toward the surface. They are not often important since most species pupate out of the water, but the Crane Fly Pupa is sometimes effective in sizes 8 to 14.

Adult crane flies may be imitated in two ways: with large, high-riding spiders and variants, and with carefully tied imitations for very choosy fish. The spiders and variants are best when buoyancy and delicacy are virtues. The realism of long pheasant-fiber legs and spent wings is best under difficult conditions.

The stiffly hackled, sparsely dressed spiders that I like to use are the Badger Spider, the Furnace Spider and the Black Spider. They are effective tied on short-shanked spider hooks in sizes 12 to 16. The hackle spread for the size 12 should be about two inches, an inch and one-half for the 14, and one inch for the 16 hook. They are deadly when skated and skipped over the surface, in the manner perfected by Edward Ringwood Hewitt for his educated Neversink trout.

The British favorite, the Red Variant, is an excellent crane fly pattern in sizes 10 and 12. It is very killing on Western streams in late summer. The Grey Fox Variant and Blue Variant are two Eastern favorites that have stood the test of time. They work well in sizes 12 and 14. An occasional smaller pattern of the Blue Variant often works wonders.

When realism is needed for some hypercritical brown trout, feather-legged crane flies of the type advocated by Bill Blades are hard to beat. These patterns are made with wings of hackle points tied spent, bodies tapered to simulate females or males, and a thickly tied thorax. The long legs are of pheasant fibers that have been knotted and tied on cleverly to suggest the legs. Excellent patterns of this type are the Blades Crane Fly and the two patterns tied by Charles Wetzel: the Whirling Crane Fly and Orange Crane Fly. The Crane Fly Quill developed by Frank Klune and myself has produced some good fish too. These flies are deadly in sizes 8 through 12. They float spraddle-legged in the surface film, and offer a tempting silhouette and tension pattern to the most supercilious trout. An occasional twitch, effected gently, makes them almost irresistible.

The angler is urged to collect and imitate his own crane fly species because the family is so numerous. The general patterns may work well enough, but local imitations may be even better.

Other common flies of the order Diptera are the little midges of the family Chironomidae. These flies are known as punkies, midges, sand flies, gnats, midgies and no-see-ums. In England the rises of trout to these tiny insects are known as smutting rises. There the little flies are called smuts and fisherman's curses.

The largest genus of this group is *Chironomus*. These little mosquito-like flies swarm over the water in large numbers from May until October. They do not bite, but a swarm of them about one's head can be highly distracting at times. The trusty briar filled with some pungent mixture is a pretty good counter-measure.

Midge Larva

The larvae are known as bloodworms and wigglers by many anglers, and are often as small as one-quarter inch in length. They have legs on the first and twelfth body segments and filament-like gills between the eleventh and twelfth body segments. Their coloring ranges from red to white.

The pupal stage has a delicate abdomen, an enlarged thorax, tiny legs and wings held close to the abdomen and hairy gills. The pupae hang vertically in the water, with the gills in the surface film. They drift along in large numbers during pupation. Imitations should be fished dead-drift, and are often effective on smutting trout. The Green Midge Pupa and White Midge Pupa are effective in size 18. Long, fine leaders are a necessity with them.

*Midge
Pupa*

Adults of the genus *Chironomus* are of many colors. They have glassy smooth wings, prominent feather-duster antennae and delicate little abdomens. They hold their front legs in the air. In this trait they are unlike the similar mosquito, which holds its rear legs in the air. The mosquito has scaly wings, unlike the smooth wings of the midge, and the female also lacks the fuzzy antennae of the midge.

The coloring of the adult midges runs from black to white, with many combinations. It is more practical to use several general flies suggestive of midges than to imitate the individual midge species.

Midge

The genus *Blepharocera* is another midge group common on fast-water streams. The larvae are dark little worms shaped like a series of black beads. They cling to the rocks in the fastest water by means of six suction cups on their undersides. Breathing is done through gills on each hairy segment. Pupae are fat and egg-shaped, with two earlike gills at the head. Their shape makes them almost impossible to imitate properly.

Adults of the genus are known as net-veined midges, and they are common on our trout streams throughout the entire season. They are not members of the family Chironomidae, but are of the family Blepharoceridae. They have glassy wings, curved bodies, a heavy thorax and long legs. Most species are very dark, and under one-quarter inch in length.

The little gnats of the genus *Hilara* are of the family Empididae. They are common on our trout water through much of the season. The larvae are wigglers quite similar to those of the genus *Chironomus,* and are found in the bottom silt. The pupal stage is also similar to that of the earlier genus. Except for glassy wings, these flies are dark blackish brown in the adult stage.

Net-Veined Midge

There are well over a thousand classified North American species of the various midge families and genera, and it is impossible and pointless to imitate them all specifically. I am recommending several patterns suggestive of midges that have proved their worth on smutting trout in the past.

Excellent larval imitations are the Claret Midge Larva, the Black Midge Larva and the Cream Midge Larva. These patterns should be tied on size 18 hooks with 2X long shanks, and fished dead-drift. Pupal imitations of the common midges are the Green Midge Pupa and Grey Midge Pupa dressed on 18 and 20 hooks with just enough gill hackle to buoy them up into the surface film.

Adult imitations are the Black Midge, Green Midge, Dun Midge, Cream Midge, Hackle Curse, Claret Smut, Badger Midge and Fisherman's Curse. They are all killing in sizes 18 through 22, fished wet or dry.

Insects of the order Neuroptera important to anglers are the alder flies and fish flies, of the family Sialidae. These species have a complete life cycle of egg, larva, pupa and adult. The pupal period is spent out of the stream and is unimportant as trout food. Alder flies are most common on slow-water stretches, while fish flies may be found in all types of water.

Larvae of the fish flies are dark brownish black, with gill filaments all along their abdomens. They live among the bottom trash, and measure from five-eighths inch to one inch in length depending upon age. The larval period is thought to last

about three years. An excellent imitation of these larvae is the
Fish Fly Larva pattern of Charles Wetzel, tied in sizes 10 to 14
with 3X long shanks. It is best when fished upstream
dead-drift.

The adult flies generally emerge from their pupal
burrows near the stream in the evening. Their general coloring consists of greyish mottled wings, greyish
legs and a cinnamon-brownish grey abdomen ringed
with dirty yellowish grey. They vary from one to two
inches in length, depending upon the stream and
species. Fish flies are often mistaken for caddis flies

*Fish Fly
Larva*

and stone flies. Imitations are best when fished semisubmerged
in the current. My favorite is the Fish Fly in size 10 with a
3X long shank. It is deadly fished dead-drift late in the afternoon and evening. On the lower Pere Marquette in Michigan

Fish Fly

there was one large old brown trout that
fell to my Fish Fly at dusk. Several floats
were offered to him with no reaction,
but he could not resist the juicy fly when
it was twitched seductively just once as
it passed his deadfall cover.

Early in the season the alder flies are over the water by the
hundreds, but it takes blustery weather to make them of real
importance. Alder flies are of the genus *Sialis,* and are quite
like caddis flies in appearance. Careful study will reveal that
they lack the little wing hairs that are characteristic of the
Trichoptera. Like the fish flies, they have a complete life cycle.
Pupation occurs out of the water and is unimportant to the
fisherman.

Alder fly larvae burrow into the bottom silt and assume
importance only when high water dislodges them. They are
quite unusual in the fact that they have a single median tail.
The thorax is a dirty yellowish grey, the abdomen is a dark
reddish brown edged with white gills, the legs are tannish and
the single tail is yellowish grey. They are from about three-
eighths to one-half inch in length. Not too much is known

about the alder fly larvae, but since one can find them in varying sizes it is likely that the larval period is about two years.

The Alder Fly Larva in sizes 12 and 14 is an excellent imitation. Naturals are found in still-water silt, and the artificial is deadly fished deep and dead-drift in such places.

Adults emerge from their pupal burrows and mate during the daylight hours. Windy weather can scatter an unimportant mating swarm into the water and cause a rise of trout. The egg masses are deposited on rocks, limbs, leaves and bridges where they

Alder Fly Larva

are over running water and in the sunlight. Each female lays two hundred to five hundred eggs in a round mass about the size of a nickel. The eggs are dark greyish brown when fresh, but two days in the sun will turn them flaky white. They are so placed that the hatching larvae fall into the stream. The females never seem to place them in a spot that is not directly over running water. The adults have brownish grey wings, brownish legs and bronzish brown bodies. The Alder Fly wet is deadly in 12 and 14.

Alder Fly

The dragonflies and damsel flies of the order Odonata are common on all ponds and streams. These insects emerge rather sporadically and are present throughout the season. Since the adult flies are large and rarely on the water, nymphal imitations are most practical. Full-grown dragonfly nymphs seem to be too large for good imitation, but imitation of partially grown specimens has worked rather well for me. Damsel fly nymphs are rather easily imitated and are important trout food. Trout seem to be rarely selective to one imitative pattern because many are present in the water at once. I have experienced one exception to this rule.

Damsel fly nymphs are easily recognized by their slender bodies that terminate in three tail-like gills. They have four thin parallel wing cases on the thorax, and large prominent eyes. They migrate from the water by crawling up a rock, plant or log and emerge in the air. Their chief value as food occurs when they are migrating, or active in the water before hatching occurs. Weedy Western streams like the Firehole in the Yellowstone country have large damsel fly populations in their weed beds.

The nymphs rarely have any formal coloring and seem to be a mottled olive-brownish. They measure from seven-eighths inch to over an inch in length. The Blades Damsel Fly Nymph and Green Damsel Fly Nymph are both good patterns, in sizes 10 and 12 with 3X long shanks. They are best when given a twitching retrieve, since the naturals are quite agile in the water.

Damsel Fly Nymph (Enallagma)

Adult imitations are sometimes effective. One of the most common genera is *Agrion,* which includes the familiar blue or green black-winged damsel flies. The abdomens are a bright metallic green or blue with lighter bands, and the wings are a deep blackish brown. The females have a touch of white at

the wing tips, and are slightly the larger. The Blue Blackwing and Green Blackwing are excellent imitations in sizes 10 and 12 with 3X long shanks.

Damsel Fly Nymph (Agrion)

Another common damsel fly group is the genus *Enallagma,* whose delicate glassy wings have a blackish mark near each wing tip. The bodies are greyish green to greyish blue in coloring. The Green Damsel Fly and Blue Damsel Fly are excellent patterns in 10 and 12, 3X long.

Trout rarely get a chance to feed upon these adult damsel flies, but windy weather and the egg-laying often give the fish an opportunity. Some species go under water on plants or logs to oviposit, and we have all seen fish leap for low-flying damsel flies. Imitations may best be fished semisubmerged in the surface film.

Dragonflies and damsel flies are often confused by anglers, but there are three easily remembered differences: dragonflies always hold their wings horizontally, while damsel flies fold their wings over their backs; most dragonflies are much larger than damsel flies; and dragonflies are more powerfully built than the fragile damsel flies. Nymphs of the dragonfly are juicy and corpulent, while the damsel fly nymphs are slender and minnow-like.

Damsel Fly

Dragonfly nymphs are highly carnivorous and range about the bottom preying upon other immature insect forms. They are generally dark green or blackish brown in coloring. The Dragonfly Nymph developed by Bill Blades is an excellent imitation in size 10, 3X long.

It was also Bill Blades who first told me of the importance of back swimmers on trout ponds in the north. These unusual little creatures are of the order Hemiptera and the family Notonectidae. They lie with the tip of the abdomen in the surface film for contact with the air, but dive and swim under water when alarmed or after prey, carrying a globule of air with them. They have sharp beaks capable of administering a nasty sting. The legs are extended when at rest and look like oars. As their name implies, they generally rest and swim upside down.

Back swimmer nymphs are smaller than the adults and have wing cases instead of the adult wings. These nymphs are highly carnivorous and even cannibalistic. The Back Swimmer   *Dragonfly Nymph* Nymph created by Bill Blades is excellent in sizes 14 and 16. It should be fished with a quick twitching retrieve, and then allowed to pause briefly.

Adults are active from spring until fall, and average about

one-half inch in length. Although the adults are capable of flight, the immature stages are the most important to the angler. Egg-laying occurs early in the season, with each female depositing about three hundred eggs. The Back Swimmer pattern tied by Blades is excellent in size 12, and should be fished like the nymph.

The little crustacea that are important as trout food are the scuds and sow bugs of the Malacostraca group. They are commonly called fresh-water shrimps by the fisherman. Waters that have large numbers of these little creatures produce heavy, red-fleshed trout that are un-equalled anywhere. Technically, these crustacea are not insects, but their imitations are nymph-like patterns. They are so important as trout food in weedy ponds and streams that I have included them here.

Back Swimmer

The scuds are of the order Amphipoda, and are found in cold water that supports plants like water cress and water moss. They are omnivorous in feeding, preferring dead aquatic life or plant forms. They are useful as scavengers as well as trout food. They rarely eat live insect forms, and this makes them far more useful as bottom-cleaners than the chubs and shiners that overrun some waters and consume large quanties of insect life. The scuds are a translucent greyish yellow and vary in size from one-quarter inch to three-quarters inch in length. The Fresh-water Shrimp is excellent in sizes 10 to 14.

Scud,
Genus Gammarus

The sow bugs are flat little crustacea of the order Isopoda. They are found in almost all waters, and can survive under adverse conditions. Adults measure from one-quarter to three-quarters inch in length and are greyish. The Grey Sow Bug is deadly in sizes 10 to 14.

These crustacea are highly prolific and often produce a brood of a dozen or more young about

Sow Bug

thirty times each year. Common scud species have bred as many as twenty thousand offspring in one year. One species of sow bug produces a new brood every two months. The hardy and prolific nature of these crustacea is appealing to men who are interested in stream rehabilitation. According to Charles Wetzel, in his book *Practical Fly Fishing,* Alex Sweigart advocates stocking streams with both trout and these crustacea, coupled with the planting of weeds to give them cover and hold the silt beds. Such projects would greatly benefit depleted water.

All anglers are familiar with the ants, of the order Hymenoptera. These are creatures that break up picnics, mar lawns with their sand homes, and drive meticulous housewives to distraction. They are terrestrial insects, but they are so common along trout streams that they contribute to the trout diet. Flying ants often swarm along and over the water, and imitations are effective. The fish can become rather selective to ant forms.

Basic coloring of these ants is brownish red to metallic black. Since both winged and wingless versions are trout foods, both types should be imitated. The Black Ant and Red Ant are excellent wet flies tied to imitate wingless ants, in sizes 10 to 14. The Black Flying Ant and Red Flying Ant are flies that may be fished dry or wet. They are deadly fished in the surface film, and are effective in sizes 10 and 14.

There are beetles of both terrestrial and aquatic nature that often form part of the trout diet. They are of the order Coleoptera and are familiar to all trout fishermen. It seems hardly necessary to describe the character of a beetle. The Brown Beetle and Black Beetle are two general patterns that have occasionally proved quite useful. They should be tied in sizes 10 to 16.

The familiar grasshopper belongs to the order Orthoptera, and is a common late-summer food of the trout. My trout fishing began with the dapping of live grasshoppers on small meadow streams. One can find an excellent dissertation on the grasshopper as a trout food in Ernest Hemingway's story,

A Way You'll Never Be. Since my graduation to the fly many seasons ago, my 'hopper fishing has been confined to artificial versions. I have found, like Hemingway in his youthful Michigan experiences, that the brownish grasshoppers have the most trout appeal. I like the dry-fly pattern known as the Michigan Hopper in sizes 8 to 14. In the larger sizes a little fox-squirrel or deer hair between the wings will help the floating qualities.

My experiences with grasshoppers have taught me three lessons valuable in fishing them: the gentle twitch of the fly, bouncing the fly off bankside grass, and dapping or swimming the fly on a short line. All of these tricks are suggestive of the natural in the water. The study of such points in the actions of both lesser and important trout foods will put weight in the creel. Or better still satisfaction, greater than any weight in the creel, in the soul of the man who has released his catch for another day.

THE STREAM DIARY

NOT ALL of the insects treated in this book are found on all of our trout waters. The local angler should use these pages as a reference guide to the insects of the streams that he frequents. We have seen how some species require fast water and others need still water. For these reasons the same insect may be important on one stream and unimportant on another that is only a few miles away.

The answer to learning local hatches is the stream diary. This book would have been impossible without the stream notes compiled by angling friends and myself. Such notes can eventually be analyzed for averages, which determine with good accuracy the habits of local species. One can find when the flies hatch, where they hatch, what weather and water conditions produce the best activity, and what local variations in coloring are found.

Insects vary in color and size from stream to stream because of temperatures, light conditions, food supplies and the chemical character of the water itself. Personal insect collections and careful diary notes are the only way to compensate for these whims of nature. The purpose of this chapter is to outline some of the rudiments of keeping the stream diary and gathering data.

The diary itself can assume any one of many physical forms, and the choice is up to the angler. The notations should be made along the stream or at the end of the day. An outline is as follows:

Location: stream, water fished, type of water, date and time spent fishing

Weather: sky, precipitation, barometer, humidity, temperatures and wind

Conditions: water level, clarity, temperatures and general character

Hatches: species, stage of development, time of hatching, temperature of water, type of water, character of hatch and weather during the hatching activity

Fishing: feeding activity, time, characteristics, rise types, type of water, successful flies, methods used, fish taken and the results of stomach autopsies

The instruments needed for gathering such data, other than those used for insect study, are a common thermometer, a stream thermometer, and access to barometric readings and humidity reports. Records of air temperatures and conditions may be available through news sources. The stream temperatures must be taken by the angler.

Many anglers will consider this just unnecessary trouble, but the data recorded are invaluable. After several years of compiling such notes on a given stream, one can begin to draw parallels that are priceless. One can construct accurate hatching calendars and predict activity.

The appearance of a new insect can be exciting and frustrating to an angling entomologist. One of the most outstanding examples of this in my notes occurred on the famous Frying Pan Creek. Showering flights of caddis flies were moving upstream into the wind each evening, and all of our attempts to match them were of no effect. We had been able to take a few small fish, but the big trout were pretty humbling as they gorged themselves and ignored our flies. The naturals appeared quite yellowish in the late afternoon sun, and we spent our nights tying little ginger and honey flies in size 16. This was our dangerous basic assumption—that the flies were yellowish. We had not yet bothered to take specimens for study.

Four days passed, with the big browns rolling steadily each evening, and our total catch was six trout including one twelve-inch rainbow. On the fifth evening I was standing helplessly in the tail of Seven Castles Pool while the big fish rose all around me. It was extremely frustrating, and I was about to quit in disgust. One of the little caddis flies flew past me, and I caught it with a savage sweep of my hand. Much to my chagrin it was a dark mottled brownish grey. But it looked yellow in the air!

I imprisoned the little insect in one of my fly boxes and searched frantically through my flies. There was a single fly in the corner of my "odd box" that had been given to me in Michigan earlier that year. It was called the Michigan Mosquito, and had brown and grizzly hackle with a peacock quill body, two long pheasant tails, and grey mallard primary wings tied down over the back like a wet fly. I quickly chopped the tails off and tied it on.

Three large fish seemed to be working about sixty feet above me in the glassy water. They were rising with big, showy swirls that left washtub-sized rings in the water. One other fish was working off to the right, making much smaller rings. In that quiet water I decided to take the largest fish first, since the ensuing struggle would put the rest down for some time. My cast straightened out nicely over the water, and then was shifted by a sudden wind to fall in a perfect hook in front of the smallest fish. He rose with sedate little swirl, and I set the hook with some disappointment. The rod doubled over into a tight arc as the fish bored deep into the pool. The throbbing bamboo spelled size, and I began to play him gingerly. After several minutes I netted an eighteen-inch brown, wondering like all anglers just how large the other fish had been. I never found out, for the battle put all of the other feeders down, and they did not rise again while I was there.

Several months later the little caddis flies were identified as *Cheumatopsyche gracilus,* and the modified Michigan pattern was named the Dark Caddis Quill. This completed my stream notes, and a valuable lesson was preserved there in the recorded data.

The study, collection and imitation of stream life is a fascinating part of fishing. It sharpens the senses of observation to a fine degree. Both the knowledge gained and the whetted powers of apprehension are of value. The gear needed to study stream insects is not complex. It may be divided into three categories: for collection, for observation and for preservation.

One can use several methods of capturing the insects. Entomologists usually are interested only in the adult males and often use a net to catch them in flight. Since anglers are already burdened with a great deal of trouting paraphernalia, the addition of a butterfly net to the load is of questionable merit. Anglers usually rely on their hands to catch insects. For nymphs and larvae that are found on rocky bottoms this method is very effective. One can pick up the rocks and remove the nymphs and larvae quite easily. Strainers made of fine screen are most useful for collecting immature burrowing forms, catching insects dislodged by moving rocks, or gathering those from weedy growths. Insects that are resting on rocks or leaves are usually easy to collect with the hands. Flying forms may be caught with the hands if one can develop the sense of timing needed. Mating May flies are quite wary when in flight, and one must stand perfectly still. They will fly within reach of a motionless angler, but will remain just out of range if he chases them. In using the hands to collect insects, one should avoid mashing or injuring the specimens. Reasonable care is sufficient.

The common kitchen strainer is an excellent tool for picking up drifting insects. The water flows through, allowing the quarry to flow into the meshes. It is very difficult to pick flies off the current by hand, and requires a fine sense of timing.

The strainer is recommended for the man with sluggish reflexes.

Two types of bottles are needed for stream collection: one for killing the specimens, and another for preserving May fly duns alive. The killing jar need not be large, and I have found ten parts rubbing alcohol and one part vinegar to be a good preservative and color-set. So much of the fluid is lost from collecting jars that I do not advise a more permanent mixture. The live duns should be allowed to moult to the spinner stage. Then one has definitely correlated the two stages, and can send the spinners to the entomologists for definite identification. Since most of the naturals are classified in the imago stage only, this is very important. The killing bottle is also used for nymphs and larvae collected.

Insects collected and placed in the killing jar on the stream should be transferred into preservation vials back at the base camp. Spinners that have been allowed to moult in the larger jar with a perforated lid should be preserved in alcohol soon after moulting. Color notes should be made quickly, as color fades. Specimens should be labeled with the name of the insect, date collected and place collected. Four parts ethyl alcohol to one part distilled water is an excellent permanent preservative.

Some angler may like to raise and study nymph life. Several pieces of equipment are necessary. For many nymphs and larvae the ordinary aquarium will do nicely, but the fast-water species require a fine-screen cage anchored in the actual stream. This is easier than an elaborate laboratory reproduction of stream conditions. When the specimens are removed for careful study, a large white plate makes an excellent background for details.

Several methods may be used for identification of the specimens. A small hand magnifying glass is useful for close work, and when one has a monograph of the various orders available he can do rather well. Clues may be gained from the habits, markings, coloring or configuration. Actual identification might best be left to the specialists in the field, and the Division of Insect Identification and Detection of the Department of Agriculture in Washington, D.C., might be the best place for final determination of exact species.

The color-photography addict can make excellent use of his projector, for glass slide mounts may be used for careful study of the wings. The wings should be mounted between two slides of clean glass and then projected on the screen, greatly enlarged. Veins and markings can easily be traced to obtain an accurate enlargement for study.

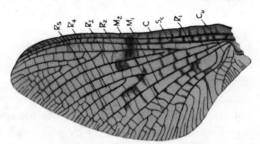

Slide Drawing of Ephemera May Fly Wing

Veins in the wings of an aquatic insect have the same basic pattern regardless of species, with six principal ones running through the wing structure: the C or costa, Sc or subcosta, R or radius, M or media, Cu or cubitus and A or anal. When these veins are repeated in a species they are designated with subnumerals numbering from front to rear. Cross veins connect these primary veins in complex and varied patterns. The enlargements of the slide-mounted wings can easily be marked with these venation symbols for study.

In sending specimens to a specialist, one might also include enlargements of venation to aid in the identification. It is important that males be sent, since most data are based upon the anatomy and venation of the adult males. The scientist is often interested in the specimens of anglers and will sometimes retain certain species to complete a collection. It is advisable to send as many data on a species as possible.

Two small points may be of some aid to the angler studying entomology: the symbols used for sex of a species, and the metric conversion unit. Males are designated by the symbol ♂ and females by the symbol ♀. The metric conversion is 25.4 millimeters equal one inch.

Some interesting work has been done with regard to anglers and insects. In the recent book, *Fun With Trout*, Fred Everett describes the successful transplanting of larger drakes to barren streams. Alvin Grove mentions a similar project in *The Lure and Lore of Trout Fishing*. This transplanting of May flies is a facet of stream improvement that has not been deeply explored. Perhaps one day our conservation departments will be stocking aquatic insects along with the fish themselves.

In an earlier chapter the observation of nymphs as an indication of hatching activity was mentioned. I once fished a small meadow stream in Colorado for several weeks and enjoyed some excellent fishing by using this trick. We shall leave the stream unnamed because it cannot stand much fishing pressure. Some of the water of the stream was diverted for irrigation of the meadows by ditches, which contained a fair representation of the fly life present.

PLATE FOUR: MAY FLIES *(opposite)*

Stenonema vicarium female spinner; *Stenonema fuscum* male spinner; *Paraleptophlebia mollis* male spinner; *Ephemera guttulata* male spinner; *Ephemerella attenuata* female spinner.

Ephemera guttulata female spinner; *Isonychia bicolor* female spinner; *Leptophlebia johnsoni* male spinner; *Leptophlebia johnsoni* female spinner; *Hexagenia recurvata* male spinner.

Hexagenia recurvata female spinner; *Stenonema canadense* female spinner; *Potamanthus distinctus* male spinner; *Potamanthus distinctus* female spinner; *Stenonema ithaca* male spinner.

Ephemerella needhami female spinner; *Siphlonurus quebecensis* male spinner; *Siphlonurus quebecensis* female spinner; *Callibaetis fluctuans* male spinner; *Epeorus longimanus* male spinner.

Epeorus longimanus female spinner; *Ephemerella infrequens* male spinner; *Ephemerella infrequens* female spinner; *Callibaetis americanus* male spinner; *Ephemerella grandis* female spinner.

Hexagenia limbata male spinner; *Hexagenia limbata* female spinner; *Epeorus albertae* male spinner; *Epeorus albertae* female spinner; *Ephemera varia* female spinner.

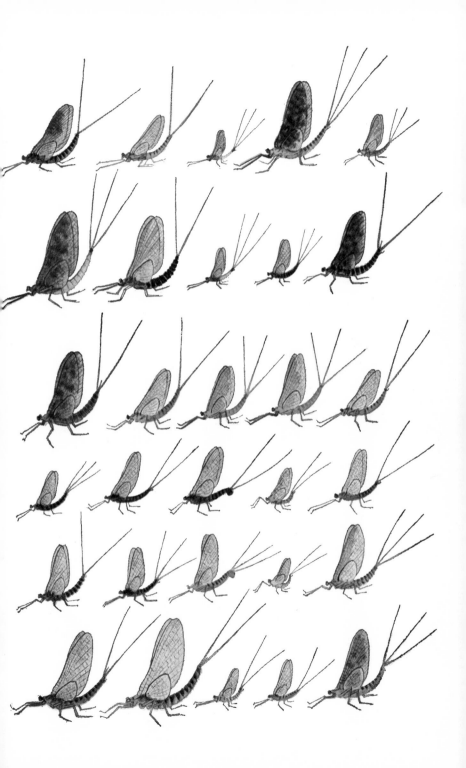

By watching the nymphs in the ditch that ran near the ranch house, I could predict hatches on the main stream fairly well. When a nymph species developed darkening wing cases, I would prepare a few adult imitations. Hatching in the ditch would send me about a mile across the meadows to the main stream. Then I would fish back to the ranch. My stream notes show that 86 per cent of the time I found a hatch and rise in progress.

The stream diary is a source of added enjoyment as well as knowledge. Quite often I have leafed through my notes recalling the days recorded. It is a bonus to the fishing, and I cannot recommend it too strongly.

ON ETHICS AND PHILOSOPHY ASTREAM

IN THAT GRADUAL and satisfying progress that one makes from the status of tyro to expert, he invariably experiences a subtle transformation from fisherman to angler. This metamorphosis is complete when he has acquired such a fine degree of fishing skill that he realizes how seriously he can deplete his sport.

Every trout fisherman goes through essentially the same development, usually under the tutelage of an experienced angler. The initial stage usually is one of fishing the live baits. My father guided me toward the eventual role of fly-fishing, and I started toward that cherished goal with the floating grasshopper on a small meadow brook in Michigan. Two things make the small stream an excellent classroom for the beginner. There is no better place to learn the wariness of trout, and the splashy strike to the grasshopper dapped gently along grassy banks is not unlike the rise to the dry fly.

As all beginners should be, I was taught to creep quietly to the chosen pocket, peer cautiously through the grass and leaves, and drop my 'hopper gently above the fish. The trout were not very large, but they usually responded with a quick splash that was excellent preparation for the fly-fishing I was to begin the following year.

The transition from the 'hopper to a rather naive but effective dry-fly technique was simple. From this basic foundation I began to dabble in other methods. As my skill increased, I went through that unfortunate stage that seems to afflict us all: the desire to bring in large numbers of fish to prove my prowess. This malady is one that we all contract at one time or another, and some men never seem to overcome its ravages.

Three years after my start on that little brook, I met a kind old gentleman on the upper Pere Marquette who smilingly asked of my luck. With the bursting pride of the ten-year-old, I raised the lid of my basket to reveal fifteen trout from eight to eleven inches in length. His kindly expression soured slightly, and he asked why I had killed so many. He added that if everyone were so fortunate, there would soon be no fish left for anyone. Quick rationalization passed his criticism off as jealousy of my catch, but as I look back I see an angler mellowed with years of pleasure on the stream, and I am ashamed.

The angler does not need dead trout in his basket to feel satisfaction. He has long since proved to himself that he can catch trout, and needs no proof for his companions. He does not fear the ridicule of others, for he knows that he could fill his limit if he wished. He counts as his highest reward the number of fish put back into the stream for another day. He may bring in fish now and then if someone has expressed a desire for them, but he loves his fishing far too much to spoil it with wanton killing of the trout.

Locating a large trout is the greatest thrill for the angler, for here is an adversary worthy of his skill. He may try the fish for hours or even days without success, and still return home satisfied. As my father recently said to me in an armchair session, it is not the hundreds of fish taken that one remembers, but those few heavy trout taken or lost under difficult conditions. Just the knowledge that a big fish is present adds flavor to a pool.

Friends once told me the story of a great trout that lived

in the pool just above their cabin. Although the stream was not posted, these men improved it unselfishly with low rock dams and private planting. The water bordered by their land became the finest anywhere on the stream, and it was not long before large wild fish began to appear in its pools. One large brown became the favorite, and all of the men had raised him at least once. Several of these men had hooked and lost him, and one had actually landed and released him after finding that he measured twenty-seven inches. The fish was like an old friend. And then an outsider armed with night crawlers and twenty-pound gut took the fish under cover of high water and killed it on the spot. Without the big brown that had lived there, the magic of Cabin Pool was gone.

Beginners may ask why one fishes if he is to release his catch. They fail to see that the *live* trout, sucking in the fly and fighting the rod, is the entire point to our sport. Dead trout are just so much lifeless meat. If food is the reason for trout fishing, then the fish market is a cheaper place to obtain it. We cannot begrudge the local angler his fish, but the man who travels hundreds of miles to the stream is paying five to twenty dollars for each pound of fish. When one stops to consider his motivation in the light of economics, it becomes obvious that he fishes for the sport and not the meat.

The question of releasing trout always brings up several arguments against the practice. Most men contend that if they do not kill the fish, somebody else will. This is quite true, but they still have not lost the fun that they had. And catching a trout adds to his shyness, and may well put him beyond the reach of men less skilled than the angler who releases him. Some fishermen will grant this point, and will add that it makes them too hard to catch. This seems to be a viewpoint of laziness rather than reason. LaBranche writes in *The Dry Fly and Fast Water* that anything that makes the fish harder to catch improves the sport. The final argument left to the skeptic is that the fish die anyway. I have long since proved this false to my own satisfaction.

In a two-week experiment on a small ranch pond I caught and released the trout. There were about thirty trout from ten to twenty inches. Each fish gave up a particular part of his dorsal or caudal fin, and the exact nature of this surgery was recorded in a notebook. Each fish had his own page, complete with data regarding his capture. Not one fish died from my handling, and many of them were taken several times each week. The fish were not handled with wet hands, for the danger of squeezing them too tightly with wet hands is greater than the threat of fungus. They were held gently in the water in a natural swimming position until they darted off in their own time. This is the only way to release trout, for the tired fish thrown carelessly back into the water may never recover his equilibrium. In the stream, one should hold them gently with their heads into the current while they recover. Catching and releasing these fish did not impair their energy in any way. They did become increasingly difficult to catch.

I have seen men who thought themselves outdoorsmen point with pride to washtubs full of small trout on Western rivers where the limit in pounds, if one wished to take it, was possible in three or four fish. In a cursory check of various state laws, I found that the highest resident and nonresident license fees are less than five and eleven dollars. When one stops to consider the fact that it costs from one to two dollars for each pound of trout stocked, he cannot help but see that the license fee does not pay for the propagation of the fish so taken. The fish hog costs us money and cuts down future sport for himself as well as others. Aside from the economic considerations, the problems boil down to pure ethics. As William Michael aptly phrased it in *Dry-Fly Trout Fishing*, it becomes a matter of "catch your limit or limit your catch." The latter course is our only choice if we are to leave anything but memories for our children.

There are many opinions on just what good trout fishing is. One school of thought may expound the virtues of wilderness water, while another quietly loves the intriguing and difficult sport of fooling a nice fish or two from some intimate "fished-out" stream. The thrill of the home run would be lost if one were hit with each trip to the plate, and so it is with fishing. The most satisfying fishing of all comes on the quiet pools of a familiar stream. This fishing in the shadow of the city is not for the man who needs weight in the creel, but a deep satisfaction comes with even a modicum of success on such water.

Farsighted individuals have shown us the way to better fishing, but it is regrettable that many of our streams have deteriorated to the point where posted water has been forced into being. We have no one to blame but ourselves. Some of the private water in our Eastern trout country is well worth serious study. The reduction in bag and size limits, and the practice of stream improvements, have greatly improved the fishing.

Edward Ringwood Hewitt has shown us how to rejuvenate unproductive water with low dams. His water on the Neversink is well known to trout fishermen. The old maestro has up his sleeve many such tricks, which may be found in his little book *Better Trout Streams*. In 1954 a log dam about three feet high was placed across a barren shallow flat on the East Branch of the Ausable in New York. On water that was formerly fit for nothing but small fish, there is now some good sport. That same season I took a nice dry-fly brownie from below this dam, and on my last evening I hooked and lost a beautiful fish that slid from beneath the foam to seize my floating Hendrickson.

Art Flick expressed some interesting ideas on stream improvement to me one season. He believes that it is useless to plant fish in streams that can no longer support wild fish in good numbers. Many anglers feel that one wild fish is worth several of his liver-fed relatives, and Art seems to think that the rivers could be reclaimed at less expense than is incurred in planting. Some of our Eastern streams are in bad shape, and some radical changes are needed. Under our present methods, the fishing gets worse each season.

Another excellent step in reclaiming our rivers is the planting of water plants to hold the silt beds. They anchor the bottom and banks in high water and serve as shelter for a myriad of aquatic forms. Weeds also greatly increase the oxygen content of the water and lower its carbon dioxide concentration through photosynthesis, and all this makes for a heavy and healthy trout population. Perhaps the primary reason for the fat, healthy fish of European rivers is the presence of the weeds. Of course the alkalinity of the chalk streams is important too, but the oxygen and fly life created and sheltered by the plants is important.

We can learn much from the Europeans about conservation. There, spinning is outlawed on water best suited to the artificial fly. Perhaps on our rivers the easily waded water should be restricted to the fly fisherman. The big, heavy water could be the beat of the spinning man, and the small brushy brooks or big water could be open to bait. Perhaps these things could be done, but the suggestions are usually met with great opposition. "It is not democratic, but serves the needs of the fly-fishing elite." Yet while these arguments of principle wear on, the fishing deteriorates.

New York restricted a few miles of its great mileage of trout water to fly-fishing only, and the uproar was almost deafening. One warden complained to me that he could not enforce the fly-fishing rules because the local magistrates refused to recognize them. Such measures have never been necessary in the past, but they are needed now. Let us hope that it is not yet too late.

If we are to continue stocking the streams with quantities of fish, perhaps we should use the European system of closing freshly stocked stretches for a season. By the second year the trout are acclimated and show the wariness of wilder fish. It is certainly no sport to take hatchery fish that have just been released. Closing water does not pay off in quick put-and-take dividends, but its benefits would be felt in later seasons. Many European rivers have stretches that lie fallow in alternate seasons. Then nature is allowed to rebuild itself without fishing pressure. The fallow water recovers quickly and serves as a constant reservoir of trout for the rest of the stream.

All of these measures would improve the fishing, but the greatest improvement of all would be an enlightened clan of anglers who practice a personal brand of ethics and regulations well within the maximum set by law. If there were more men who followed the credo of "limit your kill," the fears for the future would be unfounded. As an embittered conservationist once said to me, "The trouble is that there are too many fishermen and too few sportsmen."

Many satisfying things are to be found along trout water, and on hard-pressed streams they help to compensate for the lack of fish. These things were viewed as streamside distractions by William Schaldach in the exquisite book *Currents and Eddies*. It is true that the sensitive angler remembers not only the trout taken or lost, but also the little things along the streams. I can remember distractions like the scores of ducks and geese on a Yellowstone pond, the intense blue of the Wyoming sky on those crisp September mornings, and the doe and fawn that crossed a Boardman riffle at twilight in Michigan. There was the mother bear with cubs that crossed the Madison in Montana, and the memory of a three-pound brown that fell to my dry fly on the Ausable is pleasantly mixed with the whippoorwills on those Adirondack ridges. And a scoreless evening in the Catskills was saved by the balmy pine-scented wind that swept down the valley just at dusk.

All of these things mean as much as the fishing itself, and such a love of trout country prompted Reuben Cross to dedicate *Fur, Feathers and Steel* * "to those anglers who never become so engrossed in their art of casting and killing trout that they cannot pause to listen to the song of a warbler or admire the beauty of a delicate wild flower . . ."

---

* Copyright 1940 by Dodd, Mead & Company, Inc.

The subject of etiquette along the stream is difficult, for I hesitate to preach about sins that have been mine in the past. Breaches of courtesy on the stream these days are all too common. The regard for the rights of others is of primary concern, and the inconsiderate fellow who shoulders in when you have taken a fish, wades through the water you are fishing, or proceeds to cast over the fish that you are working, is a thoughtless boor.

The real sportsman does not hesitate to dress his share of the trout or to scour the dirty dishes in the sand. He helps the less-experienced angler in any way that he can and does not fear the competition that may result. There is a brotherhood among anglers. Some of my closest friends were met casually along a trout stream many miles from home. There is no caste system on trout water. The fish will rise to the crude fly dapped by the backwoods native as well as to the dainty imported one cast by the wealthy financier.

Specific rules in angling etiquette are few, and common courtesy is the basis. It is poor form to enter a stream not far above another if he is fishing in that direction. The skillful angler does not disturb the water much, but the beginner is likely to frighten the fish and put them down for some time. One should realize his own capabilities, and enter the stream at a discreet distance above or below another man. The first man in the river has the right of way, and we must not disturb his fun.

Often I have raised a good fish and have retired to the bank to rest him. Resting a pool or run is the same as fishing it in stream etiquette. Approaching anglers should bypass such water, or ask if it is being rested, before fishing.

As a matter of tradition the man wading upstream has the right of way, since the man coming down is more likely to spoil the former's chances. The one wading down should retire from the water and move unobtrusively around him. Often the inconsiderate fisherman will acknowledge the right of way and then wade noisily past or walk along in plain view of the fish. He is certainly not improving his own sport, and he is ruining the fishing of another.

I once fished a quiet stream with one of the noisiest waders I have ever known. The river was small and flowed gently though pines and cedars over a sandy bottom. The fish were not large, but it was pleasant work. On a placid willow-and-cedar-shaded run one evening, I was startled by a cowlike sloshing behind me. This gentleman had stepped off a low bank into two feet of water, announcing that he was ready to go because there were no trout in the stream. He waddled up to me with the stride used on Manhattan sidewalks, and the surflike waves that rolled up the quiet run can be easily imagined. The trout did not rise again that evening.

Much of the water we fish is bordered by private property, and we should respect it. Cattle can be easily frightened and stampeded by the thoughtless angler, with a resultant loss in weight or chance of injury. One ill-tempered bull can right many wrongs here.

Some landowners who allow fishing build gates or stiles for fishermen to cross their fences, but there is always some anarchist who carries wire-cutters or pliers to pull the staples. We can hardly blame the owners of posted land in many instances.

The cardinal sin so often committed is the disfiguring of the water or the land along it. The refuse that litters the stream and adjacent campsites is often quite astonishing. I have seen bedsprings, cans, bottles, tires, golf clubs and other junk in trout streams. I once caught a nice brown that came from under a transient toilet seat to take my nymph. The logs and stumps of nature would have been a much more pleasing setting. And there is something sacrilegious about cans and bottles in the Beaverkill, and the heavy truck tire that lies deep in Seven Castles Pool on the Frying Pan. What illness of the mind causes this?

Trout fishing at its best is a gentle art, both humbling and satisfying. Many who pursue it never see the subtle side at all, but those who do are never without rich memories and the deep satisfaction that comes with anything well done.

Izaak Walton wrote in 1653: "He that hopes to be a good angler must not only bring an inquiring, searching, observing wit; but he must also bring a large measure of hope and patience."

In these days of hard-fished waters, ethics and philosophy play an ever increasing role in our enjoyment, and to Father Walton's measure of hope and patience let us add the spice called charity.

AFTERWORD

THINK BACK through your fishing to a favorite pool. Its surface is covered with the swirls of trout rising to the hatch. You make a quiet approach and execute a perfect cast. The fly rides naturally with no sign of drag. But there is no response. The hatch is heavier now, and the water boils with rises. The fly box is exhausted of alternatives as you change flies in desperation, but the rise is over before you succeed in matching the hatch and you wade sadly from the river.

Very few anglers are much concerned with the insects that emerge from their favorite trout streams, but the study of those insects is the key to successful fly-fishing. Several years ago I encountered an angler who was concerned with trout-stream insects. We met in the midst of magnificent scenery in the shadow of Mount Massive in Colorado. As I hailed him along that mountain stream, he was just placing an insect in a collection jar. With a studied nonchalance fed on many seasons astream, I examined the flies tied by my new acquaintance, but my attitude of indifference changed quickly as I saw the lifelike patterns and the exquisite tying.

From that moment many years ago on a Colorado brook I have been greatly indebted to the author of this book. He is the angler that I met in those high mountain meadows. As is so typical of trout fishermen, we have been fast friends ever since that chance meeting of long ago.

This fly-fishing entomologist has successfully correlated effective patterns with the hatches found on the streams of our country. He has so thoroughly collected the important hatches of my region that I treasure the wealth of data gained for the Colorado angler.

The guidance in these pages is the result of many years of study. It represents countless hours of pleasure spent on hundreds of streams, both in this country and in Europe, catching trout and collecting insects, plus toil with fur and feathers in widespread camps and cabins. I am proud of the part that I played, for we were together when some of the patterns were born in his vise, and later we fished these dainty creations on many Western rivers with deadly effects.

This is not a complete guide to insect life on the streams of our country, and the author will be the first to tell you that. I believe that it is more complete than any other work of its kind thus far. It helps to solve many of the mysteries of fly-fishing for those who will study it diligently. Here is a wealth of trout lore at your finger tips. The angler mastering it would do well to study the last chapter thoroughly so he will not abuse the knowledge gained.

FRANK E. KLUNE, JR.

Leadville, Colorado

APPENDIX

Hatching Charts and Fly Patterns

PERHAPS THE HARDEST task facing the man who attempts to write on fishing entomology is the compilation of a workable set of hatching charts. No matter what system is selected, the charts cannot be as complete as one would like to make them, and they will have their limitations for the man using them in his fishing.

There are many admirable ways of arranging emergence data. Perhaps the easiest is to neatly sidestep the entire question, and give selected dates upon which certain hatches have appeared on certain streams. Although such data would constitute a real contribution to trout lore, they do not answer the needs of an angler trying to use them on the stream. Beginners might expect to find the hatch listed emerging on the date listed.

The system of giving a popular name for the hatch followed by distribution and initial hatching dates also has its advantages. Yet there are many popular names floating around, such as Blue Dun, Green Drake and Yellow May. There are so many for each species that it has got to the point where anglers cannot converse intelligently with others when they fish away from home. The reason is rather simple. One man's Green Drake is another man's Shad fly, depending upon the region in which he lives. If the man from the Beaverkill and the man from Penn's Creek both called the hatch *Ephemera guttulata,* they would be on less boggy ground. The biologists faced this confusion long before it filtered down to the angler, and the result was the Latin designation used by all. There is no way to sugar-coat these scientific names and still avoid the confusion that surrounds local and popular names.

Many items were considered for the hatching charts, and many were discarded. When I attempted to set up an ideally complete chart, I realized that it was impossible to put all of the information contained in these pages into a chart that could fit into the book.

An inspired solution by Jeff Norton was the answer to the hatching calendar. His amazingly simple bar-graph suggestion not only shows when an insect is present, but also shows how the hatchings overlap. This overlapping of emergence is difficult to explain, and I think that the graphic approach is worth thousands of words.

Barring an extremely early or late season, the Eastern calendar is fairly accurate. The Western calendar has variable limitations imposed by altitude. I offer both with no little trepidation, fully realizing their possibilities and shortcomings. I am resigned to weathering the scorn of the first fisherman who confidently wades into his favorite stream and does not find a hatch.

All statistics are based upon averages obtained by considering early and late exceptions. Contrary to the famous Disraeli outburst, "There are lies, damned lies and statistics," there is some merit in these charts. The angler may use them to narrow down the possible identities of the hatch he has encountered. From that point, he can use the detailed discussions found in the text.

I make no attempt to add to the countless pages of excellent material on fly-tying. The basic techniques are common knowledge to many anglers. Beginners should study such thorough work as Cross' *The Complete Fly Tyer* or Blades' *Fishing Flies and Fly Tying.* These books cover the fundamentals for expert and neophyte alike. For the man who does not tie his own flies, the patterns in the appendix can be reproduced by any competent fly-tier.

The hook sizes throughout the book have been given only as a numbered size. Since there is such a wide variation from manufacturer to manufacturer, perhaps it is best that specific brands and models be recommended for the various lures. The May flies are imitated in three stages: nymph, dun and spinner. The nymphs and wet-fly spinners are tied on Mustad wet-fly Model Perfect hooks with 2X long shanks. The dry-fly imitations are on Bergman Nyack Model Perfect hooks with 2X fine wire. Wet-fly duns are tied on Mustad Model Perfect hooks. Caddis fly and stone fly imitations are on Mustad Model Perfect hooks with 2X long shanks. Dry-fly imitations of these orders are on Bergman hooks with 2X fine wire. Since the size of insects varies from stream to stream with water conditions, the exact hook sizes are not too important to an angler concerned with local waters. He must exercise his own judgment with regard to native species.

Armed with the right fly pattern in the right size and a thorough briefing on the nature of the hatch, the angler can return to the contest with vigor. In knowledge there is strength.

Natural and Artificial Correlation: Eastern May Flies

Genus and Species	Tails	Water Type	Stage	Activity	Artificial	Dry	Wet
Epeorus pleuralis	2	Fast	Nymph	Noon	Epeorus Nymph No. 12–14–16		x
		Medium	Dun ♂	1:30 P. M.	Dark Gordon Quill No. 14	x	
			Dun ♀	1:30 P. M.	Gordon Quill No. 12	x	
					Hare's Ear No. 12–14		x
		Fast	Imago ♂	Midday	Red Quill Spinner No. 14	x	x
Page No. 37			Imago ♀	Midday	Female Red Quill Spinner No. 12	x	x
Paraleptophlebia adoptiva	3	All	Nymph	Morning	Leptophlebia Nymph No. 16–18	x	
			Dun ♂	11:00 A. M.	Dark Blue Quill No. 20	x	
			Dun ♀	11:00 A. M.	Dark Red Quill No. 18	x	
			Imago ♂	Midday	Blue Quill Spinner No. 20	x	x
Page No. 40			Imago ♀	Midday	Female Blue Quill Spinner No. 18	x	x
Iron fraudator	2	Fast	Nymph	Noon	Iron Nymph No. 12–14	x	
		Medium	Dun ♂	1:30 P. M.	Dark Gordon Quill No. 14	x	
			Dun ♀	1:30 P. M.	Hare's Ear No. 12–14		x
					Gordon Quill No. 12	x	
		Fast	Imago ♂	Midday	Red Quill Spinner No. 14	x	x
Page No. 42			Imago ♀	Midday	Female Red Quill Spinner No. 12	x	x

Genus and Species	Tails	Water Type	Stage	Activity	Artificial	Dry	Wet
Ephemerella subvaria	3	All	Nymph	1:00 P. M.	Dark Ephemerella Nymph No. 12–14		x
Ephemerella rotunda			Dun ♂	2:00 P. M.	Red Quill No. 14	x	
Ephemerella invaria			Dun ♀	2:00 P. M.	Hendrickson No. 12	x	
			Imago ♂	Midday	Little Rusty Spinner No. 14	x	x
			Imago ♀	Midday	Female Hendrickson No. 12	x	
Page No. 43					Female Beaverkill No. 12		x
Leptophlebia cupida	3	Slow	Nymph	Noon	Dark Leptophlebia Nymph No. 10–12		x
			Dun ♂	2:00 P. M.	Black Quill No. 14	x	
			Dun ♀	2:00 P. M.	Whirling Dun No. 12	x	
			Imago ♂	Midday	Black Quill Spinner No. 14	x	x
Page No. 47			Imago ♀	Midday	Early Brown Spinner No. 12	x	x
Stenonema vicarium	3	Fast	Nymph	Sporadic	Dark Stenonema Nymph No. 10–12		x
	2	All	Dun ♂ ♀	Sporadic	American March Brown No. 10–12	x	
Page No. 50		Fast	Imago ♂ ♀	Evening	Great Red Spinner No. 10–12	x	x
Epeorus vitrea	2	Fast	Nymph	Evening	Iron Nymph No. 16		x
		Medium	Dun ♂	Evening	Little Sulphur Dun No. 18	x	
			Dun ♀	Evening	Pale Watery Dun No. 16	x	
					Little Marryatt No. 16–18		x
		Fast	Imago ♂	Evening	Pale Watery Spinner No. 18	x	x
Page No. 55			Imago ♀	Evening	Ginger Quill Spinner No. 16	x	x

Genus and Species	Tails	Water Type	Stage	Activity	Artificial	Dry	Wet
Ephemerella dorothea	3	All	Nymph	Evening	Ephemerella Nymph No. 14–16		x
			Dun ♂	Evening	Little Marryatt No. 16	x	
			Dun ♀	Evening	Pale Watery Dun No. 14	x	
			Imago ♂	Evening	Male Pale Evening Spinner No. 16	x	x
Page No. 57			Imago ♀	Evening	Pale Evening Spinner No. 14	x	x
Stenonema fuscum	3	Fast	Nymph	Sporadic	Stenonema Nymph No. 12		x
	2	All	Dun ♂ ♀	Sporadic	Grey Fox No. 12–14	x	x
Page No. 59		Fast	Imago ♂ ♀	Sporadic	Ginger Quill Spinner No. 12–14	x	x
Paraleptophlebia mollis	3	All	Nymph	Morning	Leptophlebia Nymph No. 16–18		x
			Dun ♂ ♀	Sporadic	Dark Blue Quill No. 18–20	x	
			Imago ♀	Evening	Blue Quill Spinner No. 18	x	
Page No. 61			Imago ♂	Evening	Jenny Spinner No. 20	x	
Ephemera guttulata	3	All	Nymph	Evening	Dark Ephemera Nymph No. 8–10		x
			Dun ♂	Evening	Male Green Drake No. 10	x	
			Dun ♀	Evening	Female Green Drake No. 8	x	
					Grey Fox Variant No. 10	x	
			Imago ♂	Evening	Male Coffinfly No. 10	x	
Page No. 63			Imago ♀	Evening	Female Coffinfly No. 8, White Wulff No. 8		x

Genus and Species	Tails	Water Type	Stage	Activity	Artificial	Dry	Wet
Isonychia bicolor	3	Fast	Nymph	Evening	Isonychia Nymph No. 10–12		x
		Medium	Dun ♂ ♀	Evening	Grey Variant No. 10–12	x	
Page No. 68			Imago ♂ ♀	Evening	White-Gloved Howdy No. 10–12	x	x
Hexagenia recurvata	3	Slow	Nymph	Evening	Hexagenia Nymph No. 8–10		x
			Dun ♂ ♀	Evening	Dark Green Drake No. 8–10	x	
Page No. 71			Imago ♂ ♀	Evening	Brown Drake No. 8–10	x	
Ephemerella attenuata	3	All	Nymph	Sporadic	Dark Ephemerella Nymph No. 14–16		x
			Dun ♂ ♀	Sporadic	Blue-Winged Olive Dun No. 14–16	x	
Page No. 73			Imago ♂ ♀	Sporadic	Blue Quill Spinner No. 14–16	x	x
Leptophlebia johnsoni	3	All	Nymph	Morning	Pale Leptophlebia Nymph No. 14–16		x
			Dun ♂ ♀	11:00 A. M.	Iron Blue Dun No. 14–16	x	
			Imago ♂	Evening	Jenny Spinner No. 16	x	
Page No. 75			Imago ♀	Evening	Blue Quill Spinner No. 14	x	
Ephemerella needhami	3	All	Nymph	Sporadic	Dark Ephemerella Nymph No. 16		x
			Dun ♂ ♀	Sporadic	Red Quill No. 16–18	x	
Page No. 77			Imago ♂ ♀	Sporadic	Little Rusty Spinner No. 16–18	x	
Stenonema canadense	3	Fast	Nymph	Sporadic	Stenonema Nymph No. 12–14		x
	2	Medium	Dun ♂ ♀	Sporadic	Light Cahill No. 12–14	x	
		Fast	Imago ♂	Evening	Ginger Quill Spinner No. 14	x	
Page No. 79			Imago ♀	Evening	Little Salmon Spinner No. 12	x	

Genus and Species	Tails	Water Type	Stage	Activity	Artificial	Dry	Wet
Hexagenia limbata	3	Slow	Nymph	Evening	Hexagenia Nymph No. 6–8		x
			Dun ♂	Evening	Dark Michigan Mayfly No. 8	x	
			Dun ♀	Evening	Light Michigan Mayfly No. 6	x	
Page No. 81		All	Imago ♂ ♀	Evening	Michigan Spinner No. 6–8	x	
Stenonema ithaca	3	Fast	Nymph	Evening	Stenonema Nymph No. 12–14		x
	2	Medium	Dun ♂ ♀	Evening	Light Cahill No. 12–14	x	
Page No. 84		Fast	Imago ♂ ♀	Evening	Ginger Quill Spinner No. 12–14	x	
Potamanthus distinctus	3	All	Nymph	Evening	Potamanthus Nymph No. 12–14		x
			Dun ♂ ♀	Evening	Paulinskill No. 12–14	x	
					Cream Variant No. 12	x	
Page No. 86			Imago ♂ ♀	Evening	Golden Spinner No. 12–14	x	
Ephemera varia	3	Slow	Nymph	Evening	Ephemera Nymph No. 10–12		x
			Dun ♂ ♀	Evening	Paulinskill No. 12–14	x	
					Cream Variant No. 12	x	
Page No. 88		Fast	Imago ♂ ♀	Evening	Yellow Drake No. 10–12	x	
Siphlonurus quebecensis	3	Slow	Nymph	Sporadic	Siphlonurus Nymph No. 10–12		x
			Dun ♂ ♀	Sporadic	Cahill Quill No. 12–14	x	
		Fast	Imago ♂	Evening	Red Quill Spinner No. 14	x	x
Page No. 91			Imago ♀	Evening	Brown Quill Spinner No. 12	x	x

Genus and Species	Tails	Water Type	Stage	Activity	Artificial	Dry	Wet
Rhithrogena impersonata	3	Fast	Nymph	Sporadic	Rhithrogena Nymph No. 12		x
	2		Dun ♂♀	Sporadic	Dark Gordon Quill No. 10–12	x	
Page No. 90			Imago ♂♀	Sporadic	Red Quill Spinner No. 10–12	x	x
Ephemerella walkeri	3	Slow	Nymph	Sporadic	Olive Dun Nymph No. 14		x
Page No. 90			Dun ♂♀	Sporadic	Olive Dun No. 14	x	
Baetis sp.	3	All	Nymph	Sporadic	Baetis Nymph No. 14–16		x
	2	All	Dun ♂♀	Sporadic	Dark Blue Quill No. 16–18–20–22	x	
			Imago ♂	Sporadic	Ginger Quill Spinner No. 18–20	x	x
Page No. 92			Imago ♀	Sporadic	Red Quill Spinner No. 16–18	x	x
Caenis sp.*	3	Slow	Nymph	Evening	Caenis Nymph No. 18		x
			Dun ♂♀	Evening	Caenis No. 18–20–22	x	
Page No. 93			Imago ♂♀	Evening	Ginger Quill Spinner No. 18–20–22	x	
Cloeon sp.*	3	Slow	Nymph	Evening	Caenis Nymph No. 18		x
			Dun ♂♀	Evening	Caenis No. 18–20–22	x	
Page No. 93			Imago ♂♀	Evening	Ginger Quill Spinner No. 18–20–22	x	
Callibaetis sp.	3	Slow	Nymph	Sporadic	Callibaetis Nymph No. 16		x
	2	Slow	Dun ♂♀	Sporadic	Grey Quill No. 16–18	x	
Page No. 94			Imago ♂♀	Sporadic	Grey Quill Spinner No. 16–18	x	

* two-winged genus

Eastern Hatching Calendar: May Flies

* Evening Hatch   ** Nocturnal Hatch

Genus and Species	April	May	June	July	August
Epeorus pleuralis					
Paraleptophlebia adoptiva					
Iron fraudator					
Baetis sp.					
Leptophlebia cupida					
Ephemerella subvaria					
Stenonema vicarium					
Ephemerella rotunda					
Ephemerella invaria					
Epeorus vitrea *					
Callibaetis sp.					
Ephemerella dorothea *					
Stenonema fuscum					
Isonychia bicolor *					
Caenis sp. *					
Rhithrogena impersonata					

Genus and Species	April	May	June	July	August
Siphlonurus quebecensis					
Ephemera guttulata *					
Paraleptophlebia mollis					
Hexagenia recurvata *					
Ephemerella walkeri					
Leptophlebia johnsoni					
Stenonema canadense *					
Ephemerella attenuata					
Stenonema ithaca *					
Ephemerella needhami					
Heptagenia sp. *					
Potamanthus distinctus **					
Cloeon sp. *					
Hexagenia limbata **					
Ephemera varia *					

173

Natural and Artificial Correlation: Western May Flies

Genus and Species	Tails	Water Type	Stage	Activity	Artificial	Dry	Wet
Cinygmula ramaleyi	3	Fast	Nymph	Sporadic	Cinygmula Nymph No. 16		x
	2	All	Dun ♂ ♀	Sporadic	Dark Red Quill No. 16–18	x	
Page No. 97			Imago ♂ ♀	Sporadic	Red Quill Spinner No. 16–18	x	x
Epeorus nitidus	2	Fast	Nymph	11:00 A. M.	Epeorus Nymph No. 10–12	x	
Page No. 99		Medium	Dun ♂ ♀	11:00 A. M.	Dark Red Quill No. 10–12	x	x
Epeorus longimanus	2	Fast	Nymph	Sporadic	Epeorus Nymph No. 12–14	x	
		Medium	Dun ♂	Sporadic	Dark Gordon Quill No. 14	x	
			Dun ♀	Sporadic	Gordon Quill No. 12	x	
					Hare's Ear No.12–14		x
		Fast	Imago ♂	Sporadic	Red Quill Spinner No. 14	x	x
Page No. 101			Imago ♀	Sporadic	Female Red Quill Spinner No. 12	x	x
Ephemerella infrequens	3	All	Nymph	Morning	Dark Ephemerella Nymph No. 12		x
			Dun ♂ ♀	Morning	Hendrickson No. 12–14	x	
			Imago ♂	Midday	Little Rusty Spinner No. 14	x	x
			Imago ♀	Midday	Female Hendrickson No. 12	x	
Page No. 103					Female Beaverkill No. 12		x

174

Genus and Species	Tails	Water Type	Stage	Activity	Artificial	Dry	Wet
Ephemerella grandis	3	All	Nymph	Sporadic	Great Red Quill Nymph No. 10		x
			Dun ♂	Sporadic	Dark Great Red Quill No. 12	x	
			Dun ♀	Sporadic	Great Red Quill No. 10	x	
Page No. 105			Imago ♂ ♀	Sporadic	Great Red Quill Spinner No. 10–12	x	x
Ephemerella inermis	3	All	Nymph	Evening	Ephemerella Nymph No. 12–14		x
Page No. 107			Dun ♂ ♀	Evening	Pale Olive Quill No. 12–14	x	
Epeorus albertae	2	Fast	Nymph	Evening	Epeorus Nymph No. 16		x
		All	Dun ♂ ♀	Evening	Pink Lady No. 16–18	x	x
		Fast	Imago ♂	Evening	Male Salmon Spinner No. 18	x	x
Page No. 109			Imago ♀	Evening	Little Salmon Spinner No. 16	x	x
Heptagenia elegantula	3	All	Nymph	Morning	Iron Nymph No. 14–16 (actual nymph unknown)		x
Page No. 111	2	All	Dun ♂ ♀	Morning	Dark Gordon Quill No. 14–16	x	
Paraleptophlebia packii	3	All	Nymph	Sporadic	Leptophlebia Nymph No. 16		x
			Dun ♂	Sporadic	Dark Blue Quill No. 18	x	
			Dun ♀	Sporadic	Iron Blue Dun No. 16	x	
Page No. 112			Imago ♂ ♀	Sporadic	Blue Quill Spinner No. 16–18	x	x
Callibaetis pallidus	3	Slow	Nymph	Sporadic	Callibaetis Nymph No. 14–16		x
			Dun ♂ ♀	Sporadic	Pale Olive Quill No. 14–16	x	
Page No. 115			Imago ♂ ♀	Sporadic	Ginger Quill Spinner No. 14–16	x	

Genus and Species	Tails	Water Type	Stage	Activity	Artificial	Dry	Wet
Stenonema verticus	3	Fast	Nymph	Sporadic	Stenonema Nymph No. 14–16		x
	2	Medium	Dun ♂ ♀	Sporadic	Paulinskill No. 14–16	x	
Page No. 116		Fast	Imago ♂ ♀	Sporadic	Ginger Quill Spinner No. 14–16	x	x
Callibaetis americanus	3	Slow	Nymph	Sporadic	Callibaetis Nymph No. 16		x
	2	Slow	Dun ♂ ♀	Sporadic	Grey Quill No. 16–18	x	
Page No. 117			Imago ♂ ♀	Sporadic	Grey Quill Spinner No. 16–18	x	x
Siphlonurus occidentalis	3	All	Nymph	Sporadic	Siphlonurus Nymph No. 10–12		x
			Dun ♂	Sporadic	Dark Grey Drake No. 10	x	
Page No. 119			Dun ♀	Sporadic	Light Grey Drake No. 8	x	
Baetis sp.	3	All	Nymph	Sporadic	Baetis Nymph No. 16		x
	2	All	Dun ♂ ♀	Sporadic	Dark Blue Quill No. 16–18–20–22	x	
					Iron Blue Dun No. 16–18–20–22	x	
					Blue-Winged Olive Dun No. 16–18–20–22	x	
			Imago ♂ ♀	Sporadic	Dark Blue Quill Spinner No. 16–18	x	x
					Ginger Quill Spinner No. 16–18	x	x
Page No. 120					Blue Quill Spinner No. 16–18	x	x

Western Hatching Calendar: May Flies

* Evening Hatch

Genus and Species	May	June	July	August	September
Cinygmula ramaleyi	■	■			
Epeorus nitidus		■	■		
Epeorus longimanus		■	■		
Callibaetis pallidus			■	■	■
Ephemerella infrequens		■	■		
Ephemerella grandis		■	■	■	■
Ephemerella inermis *			■	■	■
Epeorus albertae *			■	■	
Callibaetis americanus			■	■	■
Heptagenia elegantula			■	■	
Paraleptophlebia packii			■	■	
Stenonema verticus			■	■	
Baetis sp.				■	■
Siphlonurus occidentalis				■	■

May Fly Imitations: Nymph Patterns

Baetis Nymph
Abdomen—dubbing mixed from rabbit, beaver and red fox fur
Thorax—dubbing mixed from rabbit and beaver fur
Wing cases—grey goose primary section
Legs—dark greyish hen hackle
Tails—three greyish fibers
Ribbing—dark olive-grey cotton thread
Silk—olive

Caenis Nymph
Abdomen—dubbing mixed from rabbit and red fox fur
Thorax—dubbing of rabbit fur
Wing cases—black duck primary section
Legs—dark brown hen hackle
Tails—three dark pheasant tail fibers
Ribbing—tannish cotton thread
Silk—brown

Callibaetis Nymph
Abdomen—olive silk ribbed with bleached peacock quill
Thorax—rabbit fur dubbed on olive silk
Wing cases—mallard primary section
Legs—dark olive-grey hen hackle
Tails—three turkey primary fibers
Ribbing—bleached peacock quill, body coated with color preservative
Silk—olive

Cinygmula Nymph
Abdomen—reddish brown hackle quill, stripped
Thorax—rabbit and beaver fur mixed
Wing cases—cinnamon turkey primary section
Legs—dark brown hen hackle
Tails—three pheasant tail fibers
Ribbing—none
Silk—brown

Dark Ephemera Nymph
Abdomen—beaver fur dubbing
Thorax—beaver fur dubbing

Wing cases—black duck primary section
Legs—light brown hackles trimmed, bent to shape and set in lacquer
Tails—three light brown hackles
Ribbing—brown dyed ostrich herl trimmed off on the belly
Silk—brown

Dark Ephemerella Nymph

Abdomen—rabbit and red fox fur mixed
Thorax—rabbit and beaver mixed
Wing cases—black duck primary section
Legs—brown partridge hackle fibers
Tails—three wood-duck flank fibers
Ribbing—brown cotton thread
Silk—olive

Dark Leptophlebia Nymph

Abdomen—beaver fur dubbing
Thorax—beaver fur dubbing
Wing cases—brown mallard feather section
Legs—dark brown hen hackle
Tails—three pheasant tail fibers
Ribbing—brown saddle hackle trimmed close to the quill and off on
    the belly and back
Silk—brown

Dark Stenonema Nymph

Abdomen—rabbit and red fox fur dubbing
Thorax—rabbit fur dubbing
Wing cases—cinnamon turkey primary section
Legs—dark brown partridge hackle fibers
Tails—three dark brown mallard fibers
Ribbing—dark brown cotton thread
Silk—brown

Epeorus Nymph

Abdomen—rabbit and red fox fur mixed
Thorax—beaver dubbing
Wing cases—brown mottled turkey feather section
Legs—brown partridge hackle fibers
Tails—two wood-duck flank fibers
Ribbing—trimmed brown saddle hackle trimmed off on the belly and
    back
Silk—black

Ephemerella Nymph

Abdomen—red fox fur dubbing
Thorax—red fox and rabbit fur mixed
Wing cases—mallard primary section
Legs—light brown hen hackle
Tails—three wood-duck flank fibers
Ribbing—light brown cotton thread
Silk—olive

Ephemera Nymph

Abdomen—cream red fox belly fur dubbing
Thorax—cream red fox fur
Wing cases—mallard primary section
Legs—cream hen hackle
Tails—three cream hackle tips
Ribbing—white ostrich herl trimmed away on belly
Silk—black

Great Red Quill Nymph

Abdomen—rabbit and red fox fur mixed to dirty grey
Thorax—rabbit fur dubbing
Wing cases—grey goose primary section
Legs—dirty greyish duck hackle fibers
Tails—three brown mallard fibers
Ribbing—maroon cotton thread
Silk—brown

Hexagenia Nymph

Abdomen—rabbit and beaver fur mixed
Thorax—beaver fur dubbing
Wing cases—grey goose primary section
Legs—trimmed grey hackles bent to shape and set in lacquer
Tails—three greyish hackle tips
Ribbing—grey dyed ostrich herl trimmed off on belly
Silk—brown

Iron Nymph

Abdomen—yellow silk coated with color preservative
Thorax—rabbit and red fox fur dubbing
Wing cases—grey goose primary section
Legs—light brown partridge hackle fibers
Tails—two wood-duck flank fibers

Ribbing—greyish hackle trimmed short and off on the back and belly
Silk—olive

Isonychia Nymph

Abdomen—beaver and brown seal mixed with dark grey wool fibers
Thorax—brown seal fur and dark grey wool fibers mixed
Wing cases—black duck primary section
Legs—dark grey hen hackle
Tails—three dark grey hackle tips
Ribbing—dark brown cotton thread
Silk—black

Leptophlebia Nymph

Abdomen—peacock quill stripped and bleached
Thorax—rabbit fur dubbing
Wing cases—mallard primary section
Legs—dark grey hen hackle
Tails—three grey fibers
Ribbing—none
Silk—black

Olive Dun Nymph

Abdomen—dark olive wool and beaver fur mixed
Thorax—beaver fur dubbing
Wing cases—grey goose primary section
Legs—light brown hen hackle
Tails—three pheasant tail fibers
Ribbing—dark brown cotton thread
Silk—brown

Pale Leptophlebia Nymph

Abdomen—red fox belly fur dubbing
Thorax—red fox dubbing
Wing cases—light brown turkey section
Legs—light brown hen hackle
Tails—three light brown fibers
Ribbing—grey cotton thread
Silk—white

Potamanthus Nymph

Abdomen—rabbit and brown seal fur mixed
Thorax—brown seal dubbing

Wing cases—grey goose primary section
Legs—dark brown partridge hackle fibers
Tails—three dark brown hackle tips
Ribbing—dark brown dyed ostrich herl trimmed off leaving sides
Silk—brown

Rhithrogena Nymph

Abdomen—rabbit and brown dyed seal mixed
Thorax—brown dyed seal dubbing
Wing cases—black duck primary section
Legs—dark brown partridge hackle fibers
Tails—three brown mallard fibers
Ribbing—reddish brown trimmed hackle cut away on back and belly
Silk—brown

Stenonema Nymph

Abdomen—red fox fur dubbing
Thorax—red fox and beaver fur dubbing
Wing cases—brown mottled turkey section
Legs—light brown partridge hackle fibers
Tails—three wood-duck flank fibers
Ribbing—amber cotton thread
Silk—white

May Fly Imitations: Dry-Fly Subimago Imitations

American March Brown   (Preston Jennings)

Wings—darkly barred lemon wood-duck flank
Hackle—dark brown and grizzly mixed
Body—tannish red fox fur dubbing
Ribbing—light brown cotton thread
Tails—dark brown hackle fibers
Silk—orange

Black Quill

Wings—black hackle points
Hackle—dark blackish grey dun
Body—stripped badger hackle quill
Ribbing—none
Tails—dark blackish grey dun hackle fibers
Silk—black

Blue-Winged Olive Dun

Wings—very dark bluish grey dun hackle points
Hackle—medium bluish grey dun
Body—pale olive-yellow wool and red fox mixed dubbing
Ribbing—none
Tails—medium bluish grey dun hackle fibers
Silk—olive

Caenis (Alvin Grove)

Wings—white hackle points
Hackle—cream
Body—cream fur dubbing
Ribbing—none
Tails—white hackle fibers
Silk—white

Cahill Quill

Wings—lemon wood-duck flank
Hackle—pale bluish grey dun and light brown mixed
Body—light brown hackle quill stripped
Ribbing—none
Tails—light brown hackle fibers
Silk—white

Cream Variant

Wings—none
Hackle—cream and honey dun mixed
Body—white hackle quill stripped
Ribbing—none
Tails—cream hackle fibers
Silk—white

Dark Blue Quill

Wings—black hackle points
Hackle—very dark bluish grey dun
Body—peacock quill unbleached and stripped
Ribbing—none
Tails—dark bluish grey hackle fibers
Silk—black

Dark Red Quill

Wings—black hackle points

Hackle—very dark bluish grey dun
Body—reddish brown hackle quill stripped
Ribbing—none
Tails—dark bluish grey hackle fibers
Silk—black

Dark Great Red Quill

Wings—wood-duck flank
Hackle—dark bluish grey dun
Body—rabbit fur dubbing
Ribbing—claret cotton thread
Tails—dark bluish grey hackle fibers
Silk—olive

Dark Gordon Quill

Wings—darkly barred lemon wood-duck
Hackle—very dark bluish grey dun
Body—bleached and stripped peacock quill
Ribbing—none
Tails—dark bluish grey fibers
Silk—olive

Dark Green Drake   (Charles Wetzel)

Wings—lemon wood-duck flank
Hackle—olive-grey dun, dark grizzly and brown mixed
Body—rabbit and beaver fur mixed dubbing
Ribbing—brown cotton thread
Tails—brown hackle fibers
Silk—brown

Dark Grey Drake

Wings—brown bucktail tied upright and divided
Hackle—very dark greyish blue dun
Body—muskrat fur dubbing
Ribbing—dark brown cotton thread
Tails—dark bluish grey hackle fibers
Silk—black

Dark Michigan May Fly

Wings—brown bucktail tied upright and divided
Hackle—very dark bluish grey dun
Body—rabbit and red fox mixed dubbing

Ribbing—claret cotton thread
Tails—brown bucktail fibers
Silk—black

Female Green Drake

Wings—lemon wood-duck flank
Hackle—pale olive-grey dun, grizzly and ginger mixed
Body—pale yellow wool mixed with red fox fur
Ribbing—light brown cotton thread
Tails—ginger hackle fibers
Silk—olive

Gordon Quill (Theodore Gordon)

Wings—lemon wood-duck flank
Hackle—medium bluish grey dun
Body—bleached peacock ribbed over yellow silk coated with color
  preservative
Ribbing—none
Tails—medium bluish grey fibers
Silk—olive

Great Red Quill

Wings—lemon wood-duck flank
Hackle—medium bluish grey dun
Body—rabbit and red fox mixed dubbing
Ribbing—brown cotton thread
Tails—medium bluish grey dun fibers
Silk—olive

Grey Fox (Preston Jennings)

Wings—grey mallard flank
Hackle—light ginger and grizzly mixed
Body—red fox belly fur dubbing
Ribbing—none
Tails—light ginger fibers
Silk—olive

Grey Fox Variant (Preston Jennings)

Wings—none
Hackle—light ginger, dark ginger and grizzly mixed
Body—ginger hackle quill, stripped
Ribbing—none

Tails—ginger hackle fibers
Silk—olive

Grey Variant
Wings—none
Hackle—dark bluish grey dun and chinchilla mixed
Body—dark reddish brown hackle quill
Ribbing—none
Tails—dark bluish grey hackle fibers
Silk—black

Grey Quill
Wings—barred teal flank
Hackle—dark grizzly
Body—badger quill stripped
Ribbing—none
Tails—dark grizzly hackle fibers
Silk—black

Hendrickson   (Roy Steenrod)
Wings—lemon wood-duck
Hackle—medium bluish grey dun
Body—pinkish urine-burned red fox belly fur
Ribbing—none
Tails—medium bluish grey hackle fibers
Silk—yellow

Iron Blue Dun
Wings—black hackle points
Hackle—very dark bluish grey dun
Body—rabbit and beaver fur dubbed thin on olive silk
Ribbing—none
Tails—brown hackle fibers
Silk—black

Little Marryatt
Wings—light bluish grey hackle points
Hackle—palest ginger
Body—pinkish urine-burned red fox mixed with pale yellow wool
Ribbing—none
Tails—palest ginger hackle fibers
Silk—white

Little Sulphur Dun   (Vincent Marinaro)
Wings—medium bluish grey hackle points
Hackle—palest ginger
Body—cream red fox belly fur mixed with olive yellow wool
Ribbing—none
Tails—palest ginger hackle fibers
Silk—yellow

Light Grey Drake
Wings—brown bucktail tied upright and divided
Hackle—light bluish grey dun
Body—rabbit and red fox fur mixed
Ribbing—light brown cotton thread
Tails—light bluish grey hackle fibers
Silk—olive

Light Cahill   (Theodore Gordon)
Wings—pale lemon wood-duck flank
Hackle—pale ginger
Body—cream red fox belly fur dubbing
Ribbing—none
Tails—pale ginger hackle fibers
Silk—yellow

Light Michigan May Fly
Wings—brown bucktail tied upright and divided
Hackle—medium bluish grey dun
Body—red fox fur dubbing
Ribbing—dark brown cotton thread
Tails—brown bucktail fibers
Silk—black

Male Green Drake
Wings—darkly barred lemon wood duck
Hackle—pale olive-grey dun, grizzly and ginger mixed
Body—rabbit fur and red fox mixed
Ribbing—dark brown cotton thread
Tails—ginger hackle fibers
Silk—olive

Olive Dun
Wings—medium bluish grey hackle points

Hackle—medium olive-grey dun
Body—beaver fur mixed with olive wool
Ribbing—brown cotton thread
Tails—medium olive-grey hackle fibers
Silk—brown

Pale Watery Dun

Wings—pale bluish grey dun
Hackle—palest watery grey dun
Body—cream red fox belly fur mixed with pale yellow wool
Ribbing—none
Tails—palest watery grey dun
Silk—white

Pink Lady   (George LaBranche)

Wings—pale bluish grey dun
Hackle—light ginger
Body—pale pink cellulite floss
Ribbing—very fine gold tinsel
Tails—light ginger hackle fibers
Silk—white

Paulinskill   (Ray Bergman)

Wings—barred mallard flank
Hackle—cream
Body—cream red fox belly fur dubbing
Ribbing—very fine gold tinsel
Tails—cream hackle fibers
Silk—white

Red Quill   (Art Flick)

Wings—lemon wood-duck flank
Hackle—dark bluish grey dun
Body—medium brown hackle quill stripped
Ribbing—none
Tails—dark bluish grey hackle fibers
Silk—olive

Whirling Dun

Wings—very dark bluish grey hackle points
Hackle—medium bluish grey dun and brown mixed
Body—muskrat and beaver fur mixed dubbing
Ribbing—none

Tails—brown hackle fibers
Silk—brown

May Fly Imitations: Wet-Fly Subimago Patterns

Emerging March Brown

Wings—lemon wood duck tied down-wing over the body
Hackle—dark brown partridge fibers
Body—rough dubbing of rabbit with guard hairs and beaver mixed
Ribbing—dark brown cotton thread, fairly thick
Tails—three long pheasant tail fibers
Silk—orange

Hare's Ear

Wings—grey mallard primary, down-winged and set in lacquer
Hackle—grey partridge fibers
Body—rough dubbing of rabbit with guard hairs
Ribbing—heavy dark brown cotton thread
Tails—two long wood-duck fibers
Silk—olive

Little Marryatt

Wings—pale starling primary tied down-wing and lacquered
Hackle—palest ginger hen hackle
Body—pink urine-burned red fox fur mixed with pale yellow wool
Ribbing—none
Tails—palest ginger hackle fibers
Silk—white

Pink Lady   (George LaBranche)

Wings—pale starling primary tied down-wing and lacquered
Hackle—light ginger hen hackle
Body—pale pink cellulite floss
Ribbing—very fine gold tinsel
Tails—light ginger hackle fibers
Silk—white

May Fly Imitations: Dry-Fly Imago Patterns

Black Quill Spinner

Wings—medium bluish grey hackle points tied spent
Hackle—very dark bluish grey trimmed off on top and bottom
Body—badger hackle quill stripped

Ribbing—none
Tails—three brown mallard fibers
Silk—black

Brown Drake

Wings—white hackle points tied spent
Hackle—brown and grizzly mixed
Body—beaver fur dubbing mixed with brown dyed seal
Ribbing—yellow cotton thread
Tails—two long pheasant tail fibers
Silk—yellow

Brown Quill Spinner   (Charles Wetzel)

Wings—pale bluish grey hackle points tied spent
Hackle—medium brown
Body—bleached peacock quill
Ribbing—none
Egg Sac—pale olive wool
Tails—two long pheasant tail fibers
Silk—olive

Blue Quill Spinner

Wings—white hackle points tied spent
Hackle—pale bluish grey dun trimmed off on top and bottom
Body—bleached peacock quill
Ribbing—none
Tails—two long grey fibers
Silk—white

Dark Blue Quill Spinner

Wings—white hackle points tied spent
Hackle—dark bluish grey trimmed off on top and bottom
Body—unbleached peacock quill
Ribbing—none
Tails—two long grey fibers
Silk—orange

Early Brown Spinner (Charles Wetzel)

Wings—pale bluish grey hackle points tied spent
Hackle—medium brown trimmed off on top and bottom
Body—rabbit and beaver fur mixed dubbing
Ribbing—tannish cotton thread

Tails—three pheasant tail fibers, center tail shortened
Silk—yellow

Female Blue Quill Spinner

Wings—white hackle points tied spent
Hackle—pale bluish grey trimmed off on top and bottom
Body—brown hackle quill stripped
Ribbing—none
Tails—three grey fibers
Silk—white

Female Hendrickson

Wings—white hackle points tied spent
Hackle—pale bluish grey trimmed off on top and bottom
Body—cream fox fur mixed with yellow wool
Ribbing—tannish cotton thread
Egg Sac—yellow wool
Tails—three wood-duck fibers
Silk—yellow

Female Red Quill Spinner   (Frank Klune)

Wings—white hackle points tied spent
Hackle—medium brown
Body—bleached peacock quill with tan tip at tails
Ribbing—none
Tails—two long pheasant tail fibers
Silk—brown

Ginger Quill Spinner

Wings—white hackle tips tied spent
Hackle—palest ginger
Body—ginger hackle quill stripped
Ribbing—none
Tails—two long wood-duck fibers
Silk—white

Golden Spinner

Wings—white hackle points tied spent
Hackle—cream and honey dun mixed
Body—cream red fox fur dubbing
Ribbing—yellow cotton thread
Tails—three cream fibers
Silk—yellow

Female Coffin Fly

Wings—brown bucktail tied upright and divided
Hackle—dark bluish grey and chinchilla mixed
Body—polar bear underfur and red fox mixed
Ribbing—white cotton thread
Tails—three pheasant tail fibers
Silk—black

Great Red Quill Spinner

Wings—white hackle points tied spent
Hackle—pale bluish grey dun
Body—rabbit and red fox fur dubbing
Ribbing—dark brown cotton thread
Tails—three pheasant tail fibers
Silk—olive

Great Red Spinner   (Charles Wetzel)

Wings—white hackle points tied spent
Hackle—medium brown
Body—red fox and beaver fur mixed
Ribbing—yellow cotton thread
Tails—two long wood-duck fibers
Silk—orange

Grey Quill Spinner

Wings—white hackle points tied spent
Hackle—light grizzly trimmed off on top and bottom
Body—bleached peacock quill
Ribbing—none
Tails—two grey fibers
Silk—white

Jenny Spinner

Wings—white hackle points tied spent
Hackle—pale bluish grey dun trimmed off on top and bottom
Body—white silk tipped with three turns of rusty orange
Ribbing—none
Tails—three long white fibers
Silk—black

Little Rusty Spinner

Wings—white hackle points tied spent

Hackle—medium brown trimmed off on top and bottom
Body—brown hackle quill stripped
Ribbing—none
Tails—three wood-duck fibers
Silk—brown

Little Salmon Spinner

Wings—white hackle points tied spent
Hackle—light brown
Body—cream fox fur mixed with pink wool
Ribbing—light brown cotton thread
Tails—two light brown fibers
Silk—brown

Male Coffin Fly

Wings—brown bucktail tied upright and divided
Hackle—very dark blackish grey dun mixed with dark grizzly
Body—rabbit and red fox fur mixed
Ribbing—brown cotton thread
Tails—three pheasant tail fibers
Silk—black

Male Pale Evening Spinner

Wings—white hackle points tied spent
Hackle—pale ginger trimmed off on top and bottom
Body—cream red fox fur dubbing
Ribbing—very fine gold tinsel
Tails—three ginger fibers
Silk—white

Male Salmon Spinner

Wings—white hackle points tied spent
Hackle—honey dun
Body—rabbit and red fox mixed dubbing with three turns of rust tip
Ribbing—salmon pink cotton
Tails—two long white fibers
Silk—rusty orange

Michigan Spinner

Wings—white bucktail tied upright and divided
Hackle—ginger and grizzly mixed
Body—cream red fox and yellow wool mixed dubbing

Ribbing—light brown cotton thread
Tails—two long pheasant tail fibers
Silk—white

Pale Evening Spinner   (Charles Wetzel)

Wings—white hackle points tied spent
Hackle—palest ginger
Body—red fox fur dubbing
Ribbing—very fine gold tinsel
Egg Sac—yellow wool
Tails—three wood-duck fibers
Silk—white

Pale Watery Spinner

Wings—white hackle points tied spent
Hackle—very pale greyish dun
Body—pale yellow cellulite floss
Ribbing—very fine gold tinsel
Tails—two white fibers
Silk—white

Red Quill Spinner   (Charles Wetzel)

Wings—white hackle points tied spent
Hackle—medium reddish brown
Body—bleached peacock quill
Ribbing—none
Tails—two long pheasant tail fibers
Silk—brown

White-Gloved Howdy   (Charles Wetzel)

Wings—white hackle points tied spent
Hackle—honey dun faced with two turns of brown
Body—beaver and brown dyed seal mixed
Ribbing—dark reddish brown cotton thread
Tails—two pheasant tail fibers
Silk—white

White Wulff   (Lee Wulff)

Wings—white bucktail tied upright and divided
Hackle—medium badger
Body—polar bear underfur and a little yellow wool mixed
Ribbing—none
Tails—white bucktail fibers
Silk—white

Yellow Drake   (Charles Wetzel)

Wings—white hackle points tied spent
Hackle—pale ginger
Body—red fox fur mixed with yellow wool
Ribbing—light brown cotton thread
Tails—three wood-duck fibers
Silk—yellow

May Fly Imitations: Wet-Fly Imago Patterns

Black Quill Spinner

Wings—grey mallard primary tied down-wing and lacquered
Hackle—very dark bluish grey hen hackle
Body—stripped badger hackle quill
Ribbing—none
Tails—three long pheasant tail fibers
Silk—black

Brown Quill Spinner   (Charles Wetzel)

Wings—grey mallard primary tied down-wing and lacquered
Hackle—medium brown
Body—bleached peacock quill
Ribbing—none
Egg Sac—pale olive wool
Tails—two long pheasant tail fibers
Silk—olive

Blue Quill Spinner

Wings—grey mallard primary tied down-wing and lacquered
Hackle—pale bluish grey hen hackle
Body—bleached peacock quill
Ribbing—none
Tails—two long grey fibers
Silk—white

Early Brown Spinner   (Charles Wetzel)

Wings—grey mallard primary tied down-wing and lacquered
Hackle—medium brown hen hackle
Body—rabbit and beaver fur mixed dubbing
Ribbing—tannish cotton thread
Tails—three pheasant tail fibers, center tail shortened
Silk—yellow

Female Beaverkill

Wings—grey mallard primary tied down-wing and lacquered
Hackle—ginger hen hackle
Body—pale yellow cellulite floss
Ribbing—none
Egg Sac—yellow wool
Tails—three wood-duck fibers
Silk—white

Female Blue Quill Spinner

Wings—grey mallard primary tied down-wing and lacquered
Hackles—pale bluish grey hen hackles
Body—brown hackle quill stripped
Ribbing—none
Tails—three grey fibers
Silk—white

Female Red Quill Spinner   (Frank Klune)

Wings—grey mallard primary tied down-wing and lacquered
Hackles—medium brown hen hackle
Body—bleached peacock quill with tan tip at tails
Ribbing—none
Tails—two long pheasant tail fibers
Silk—brown

Ginger Quill Spinner

Wings—grey mallard primary tied down-wing and lacquered
Hackles—pale ginger hen hackle
Body—ginger hackle quill, stripped
Ribbing—none
Tails—two long wood-duck fibers
Silk—white

Great Red Spinner   (Charles Wetzel)

Wings—grey mallard primary tied down-wing and lacquered
Hackle—medium brown hen hackle
Body—red fox and beaver fur mixed
Ribbing—yellow cotton thread
Tails—two long wood-duck fibers
Silk—orange

Little Rusty Spinner

Wings—grey mallard primary tied down-wing and lacquered

Hackle—medium brown hen hackle
Body—brown hackle quill stripped
Ribbing—none
Tails—three wood-duck fibers
Silk—brown

Pale Evening Spinner (Charles Wetzel)

Wings—grey mallard primary tied down-wing and lacquered
Hackle—palest ginger
Body—pale yellow cellulite floss
Ribbing—very fine gold tinsel
Egg Sac—yellow wool
Tails—three wood-duck fibers
Silk—white

Male Pale Evening Spinner

Wings—grey mallard primary tied down-wing and lacquered
Hackle—pales ginger
Body—cream red fox dubbing
Ribbing—very fine gold tinsel
Tails—three ginger fibers
Silk—white

Pale Watery Spinner

Wings—grey mallard primary tied down-wing and lacquered
Hackle—very pale greyish dun
Body—pale yellow cellulite floss
Ribbing—very fine gold tinsel
Tails—two white fibers
Silk—white

Red Quill Spinner (Charles Wetzel)

Wings—grey mallard primary tied down-wing and lacquered
Hackle—medium brown hen hackle
Body—bleached peacock quill
Ribbing—none
Tails—two long pheasant tail fibers
Silk—brown

White-Gloved Howdy (Charles Wetzel)

Wings—grey mallard primary tied down-wing and lacquered
Hackle—medium brown hen hackle
Body—beaver and brown dyed seal mixed

Ribbing—dark reddish brown cotton thread
Tails—two pheasant tail fibers
Silk—white

Caddis Fly Imitations: Larval Patterns

Caddis Worm

Abdomen—polar bear underfur dubbing
Ribbing—white cotton thread
Thorax—brown seal fur dubbing
Legs—dark brown partridge fibers
Silk—black

Cased Caddis   (Oscar Weber)

Abdomen—silk base covered with sand set in glue
Thorax—brown seal fur
Legs—brown partridge fibers
Silk—black

Green Caddis Larva

Abdomen—polar bear dubbing mixed with olive-yellow wool
Ribbing—white cotton thread
Thorax—beaver fur dubbing
Legs—brown partridge fibers
Silk—black

Psilotreta Larva

Abdomen—tapered silk base covered with coarse sand in glue
Thorax—brown seal fur dubbing
Legs—brown partridge fibers
Silk—black

Stick Caddis

Abdomen—silk base covered with wood splinters and fibers in glue
Thorax—brown seal fur dubbing
Legs—brown partridge fibers
Silk—black

Caddis Fly Pupal Imitations

Dark Caddis Pupa   (Ed Sens)

Abdomen—rough grey rabbit fur dubbing

Thorax—brown seal fur dubbing
Legs—dark brown partridge fibers tied long and parallel to body
Wing cases—thin mallard primary sections tied along sides
Silk—black

Green Caddis Pupa   (Ed Sens)

Abdomen—rabbit fur mixed with olive-green wool
Thorax—brown seal fur dubbing
Legs—long grey mallard flank fibers along body
Wing cases—thin mallard primary sections along sides
Silk—black

Light Caddis Pupa

Abdomen—polar bear underfur and rabbit mixed
Thorax—rabbit fur and beaver mixed
Legs—mallard flank along body
Wing cases—thin mallard primary sections along sides
Silk—black

Caddis Fly Imitations: Adult Dry-Fly Patterns

Adams   (Leonard Halladay)

Wings—grizzly hackle points tied spent
Hackle—medium brown and grizzly mixed
Body—muskrat fur dubbing
Tails—grizzly and brown hackle fibers tied short
Silk—white

Brown Sedge

Wings—light brown turkey sections tied down-wing around hackle
Hackle—medium brown tied full at eye and palmer trimmed at sides
Body—rabbit fur and beaver mixed
Silk—rusty orange

Cinnamon Sedge

Wings—cinnamon turkey sections tied down-wing around hackle
Hackle—fiery brown tied full at eye and palmer trimmed at sides
Body—dark brown cotton thread
Silk—brown

Dark Blue Sedge   (Preston Jennings)

Wings—grey mallard primary tied down-wing around hackle

Hackle—very dark bluish grey tied palmer and trimmed at sides
Body—brown seal fur dubbing
Silk—white

Dark Caddis Quill

Wings—grey mallard primary tied down-wing
Hackle—brown and grizzly mixed at eye only
Body—bleached peacock over shaped silk base
Silk—white

Dark Brown Sedge

Wings—brown mottled turkey sections tied down-wing around hackle
Hackle—fiery brown tied palmer and trimmed at sides
Body—red fox fur dubbing
Silk—rusty orange

Female Grannom

Wings—brown mottled turkey tied down-wing around hackle
Hackle—very dark bluish grey tied palmer and trimmed at sides
Body—stripped badger hackle quill
Egg Sac—greenish yellow wool
Silk—white

Green Sedge

Wings—light mottled turkey tied down-wing around hackle
Hackle—medium brown tied palmer and trimmed at sides
Body—rabbit fur mixed with greenish yellow wool
Ribbing—brown cotton thread
Silk—yellow

Little Black Caddis   (Charles Wetzel)

Wings—black duck primary sections tied down-wing
Hackle—natural black
Body—muskrat dubbing
Silk—black

Male Grannom

Wings—brown mottled turkey tied down-wing around hackle
Hackle—very dark bluish grey tied palmer and trimmed at sides
Body—badger hackle quill stripped
Silk—white

Whitcraft   (Don Martinez)

Wings—grizzly hackle points
Hackle—brown and grizzly mixed
Body—bleached peacock quill
Tails—grizzly and brown fibers tied short
Silk—white

Caddis Fly Imitations: Wet-Fly Patterns

All of the adult caddis fly imitations may be fished wet if sparsely tied. The Adams and Whitcraft are dry-fly patterns only.

Stone Fly Imitations: Nymph Patterns

Early Brown Stone Fly Nymph

Wing cases—grey goose primary section formed into two cases
Legs—dark bluish grey hen hackle
Thorax—rabbit fur mixed with beaver
Abdomen—beaver, rabbit and brown dyed seal dubbing
Ribbing—dark brown cotton
Tails—two pheasant tail fibers
Silk—brown

Light Brown Stone Fly Nymph

Wing cases—grey goose primary section formed into two cases
Legs—brown partridge hackle fibers
Thorax—red fox dubbing
Abdomen—red fox fur dubbing
Ribbing—dark brown cotton thread
Tails—two pheasant tail fibers
Silk—brown

Yellow Stone Fly Nymph

Wing cases—pale grey feather section formed into two cases
Legs—ginger hen hackle
Thorax—cream red fox fur mixed with yellow wool
Abdomen—cream red fox fur mixed with yellow wool
Ribbing—yellow cotton thread
Tails—two ginger fibers
Silk—white

Stone Fly Nymph   (Bill Blades)

Wing cases—tan breast feathers trimmed to shape and touched with
   brown lacquer in suggestion of natural
Legs—chinchilla hackle trimmed, bent to shape and set in lacquer
Thorax—natural tan raffia grass
Abdomen—natural raffia ribbed with bleached peacock and lacquered
Tails—two ginger hackle quills
Antennae—two wood-duck fibers
Eyes—black lacquer
Silk—amber

Stone Fly Imitations: Adult Imitations

Early Brown Stone Fly   (Theodore Gordon)

Wings—grey mallard primary tied flat over the body and lacquered
Hackle—bluish grey
Body—reddish brown hackle quill
Tails—two grey fibers
Silk—brown

Giant Stone Fly   (Ed Sens)

Wings—brown mottled turkey tied flat over body and lacquered
Hackle—brown, tied palmer and full at eye, trimmed off under wing
Body—rabbit and red fox fur dubbing roughly mixed
Ribbing—yellow wool
Tails—two long pheasant fibers
Silk—brown

Western Salmon Fly   (Don Harger)

Wings—fox squirrel, one and one-half times length of body
Hackle—medium brown and dark grizzly mixed
Body—tan raffia over kapok dubbing
Tails—fox squirrel hair
Silk—brown

Little Black Stone Fly   (Charles Wetzel)

Wings—black duck tied flat over body and lacquered
Hackle—very dark blackish grey dun
Body—badger hackle quill stripped
Tails—two black fibers
Silk—black

Little Green Stone Fly

Wings—grey mallard primary tied flat over body and lacquered
Hackle—pale olive-grey dun
Body—red fox and green wool mixed dubbing
Ribbing—white cotton thread
Tails—two light green fibers
Silk—olive

Little Yellow Stone Fly

Wings—grey mallard primary tied flat over body and lacquered
Hackle—palest ginger
Body—cream red fox fur and yellow wool mixed
Ribbing—yellow cotton thread
Tails—two ginger fibers
Silk—yellow

Mallard Quill

Wings—brown mallard tied flat over body
Hackle—dark brown
Body—bleached peacock quill
Tails—two pheasant tail fibers
Silk—brown

Stone Fly   (Charles Wetzel)

Wings—mottled turkey tied flat over body and lacquered
Hackle—medium brown
Body—rabbit fur dubbing
Ribbing—yellow cotton thread
Egg Sac—yellow wool
Tails—two long pheasant fibers
Silk—white

Willow Fly

Wings—grey goose primary tied flat over back and lacquered
Hackle—brown furnace tied palmer trimmed off under wing
Body—rabbit fur and pale orange wool mixed dubbing
Tails—two pheasant tail fibers
Silk—rusty orange

Wulff Stone Fly   (Lee Wulff)
Wings—brown bucktail tied down over body

Hackle—brown bucktail fibers tied bass-bug style at the sides
Body—muskrat and red fox mixed dubbing
Tails—brown bucktail fibers
Silk—brown

Crane Fly Larval Imitations

Brown Crane Fly Larva

Abdomen—beaver and seal fur dubbing
Thorax—beaver and seal fur dubbing
Ribbing—dark brown cotton thread
Silk—brown

Green Crane Fly Larva

Abdomen—cream red fox and green wool mixed dubbing
Thorax—cream red fox and green wool mixed dubbing
Ribbing—white cotton thread
Silk—white

White Crane Fly Larva

Abdomen—polar bear underfur dubbing
Thorax—polar bear underfur dubbing
Ribbing—pale grey cotton thread
Silk—white

Crane Fly Pupal Imitations

Crane Fly Pupa

Body—polar bear underfur dubbing
Ribbing—pale grey cotton thread
Wings—long thin mallard primary sections tied along sides
Legs—long mallard flank fibers tied under body

Adult Crane Fly Imitations

Black Spider

Hackle—very dark blackish grey dun
Body—gold tinsel
Tails—dark blackish grey hackle fibers
Silk—black

Blades Crane Fly (Bill Blades)

Wings—bluish grey hackle points tied spent
Legs—knotted argus pheasant fibers

Thorax—red fox fur dubbing
Abdomen—natural raffia grass
Ribbing—fine gold tinsel
Silk—white

Badger Spider

Hackle—golden badger
Body—peacock quill
Tails—golden badger hackle fibers
Silk—black

Blue Variant

Hackle—medium bluish grey dun
Body—gold tinsel
Tails—medium bluish grey hackle fibers
Silk—yellow

Crane Fly Quill

Wings—multicolor hackle points tied spent
Legs—knotted argus pheasant fibers
Thorax—red fox and orange wool mixed dubbing
Abdomen—orange silk set with color preservative
Ribbing—bleached peacock quill under the color set
Silk—rusty orange

Furnace Spider

Hackle—brown furnace
Body—peacock quill
Tails—brown furnace fibers
Silk—yellow

Grey Fox Variant   (See May fly imitations)

Orange Crane Fly   (Charles Wetzel)

Wings—cream hackle points tied spent
Legs—light brown knotted pheasant fibers
Thorax—red fox and orange wool mixed
Abdomen—red fox and orange wool mixed
Ribbing—very fine gold tinsel
Silk—rusty orange

Red Variant

Wings—woodcock primary tied upright and divided
Hackle—brown furnace

Body—bleached peacock quill
Silk—white

Whirling Crane Fly   (Charles Wetzel)
Wings—chinchilla hackle points tied spent
Legs—knotted argus pheasant fibers
Thorax—beaver fur dubbing
Abdomen—beaver fur and green wool mixed
Ribbing—fine gold tinsel
Silk—olive

Midge Larval Imitations

Claret Midge Larva
Body—rabbit and beaver mixed dubbing dressed thin
Ribbing—claret cotton thread

Black Midge Larva
Abdomen—yellow silk
Ribbing—black ostrich herl trimmed off on back and belly

Cream Midge Larva
Abdomen—red fox fur dressed thin
Ribbing—white cotton thread

Midge Pupal Imitations

Green Midge Pupa   (Charles Wetzel)
Gill hackle—white
Thorax—red fox and green wool mixed
Legs—mallard flank fibers parallel to body
Abdomen—white hackle quill
Tail tuft—short white hackle fibers
Silk—white

Grey Midge Pupa
Gill hackle—pale greyish dun
Thorax—rabbit fur dubbing
Legs—mallard flank fibers parallel to body
Body—bleached peacock quill
Tail tuft—short grey fibers
Silk—white

Adult Midge Imitations

Badger Midge
Hackle—badger
Body—peacock quill

Black Midge
Hackle—black
Body—peacock quill

Claret Smut
Hackle—brown
Body—claret silk

Cream Midge
Hackle—cream
Body—white hackle quill

Dun Midge
Hackle—bluish grey dun
Body—yellow silk

Fisherman's Curse
Hackle—blackish grey dun
Body—brown pheasant tail fiber

Green Midge
Hackle—pale olive-grey
Body—olive hackle quill

Hackle Curse
Hackle—dark brown
Body—black silk

Alder Fly and Fish Fly Imitations

Alder Fly Larva   (Charles Wetzel)
Thorax—red fox and yellow wool mixed
Abdomen—beaver fur dubbing and brown lacquer over trimmed ostrich
Ribbing—greyish ostrich herl trimmed off on back and belly
Legs—ginger hackle
Tail—white hackle tip
Silk—white

Fish Fly Larva   (Charles Wetzel)
Thorax—muskrat and beaver fur mixed
Abdomen—muskrat and beaver fur mixed
Ribbing—dark grey ostrich herl trimmed off on belly and back
Legs—black hackle
Silk—black

Alder Fly
Wings—woodcock primary tied down-wing over back
Hackle—brown furnace
Body—peacock herl
Silk—brown

Fish Fly   (Charles Wetzel)

Wings—grey mottled turkey tied down-wing over body
Hackle—dark furnace hackle at eye
Body—muskrat and beaver mixed dubbing
Ribbing—yellow cotton thread
Silk—brown

Damsel Fly and Dragonfly Imitations

Blades Damsel Fly Nymph   (Bill Blades)

Wing cases—four grey mallard primary sections, thin
Thorax—rabbit and beaver fur dubbing
Legs—ginger hackle trimmed, bent to shape and set in lacquer
Abdomen—natural raffia marked with brown lacquer along sides
Ribbing—very fine gold tinsel under lacquer
Tails—three multicolor hackle tips
Silk—white
Eyes—black lacquer

Green Damsel Fly Nymph

Wing cases—four grey mallard primary sections, thin
Thorax—rabbit mixed with olive wool
Legs—pale greyish dun hackle trimmed, bent and lacquered
Abdomen—rabbit mixed with olive wool
Ribbing—dark olive cotton thread
Tails—three dark olive hackle tips
Silk—olive
Eyes—black lacquer

Dragonfly Nymph   (Bill Blades)

Wing cases—four brown feather sections
Thorax—thick brown dyed seal and beaver dubbing
Legs—brown hackle trimmed, bent and lacquered
Body—raffia over wool base and lacquered dark brown
Tails—four short brown fibers
Silk—brown
Eyes—black lacquer

Blue Blackwing

Wings—four black hackles tied streamer-fly style

Legs—very dark bluish grey hackle
Abdomen—blue gantron floss
Silk—black

Green Blackwing

Wings—four black hackles tied streamer-fly style
Legs—very dark bluish grey hackle
Abdomen—green gantron floss
Silk—olive

Green Damsel Fly

Wings—four light bluish grey hackles tied streamer-fly style
Legs—medium bluish grey hackle
Abdomen—light greenish silk
Ribbing—very fine gold tinsel
Silk—olive

Blue Damsel Fly

Wings—four light bluish grey hackles tied streamer-fly style
Legs—medium bluish grey hackle
Abdomen—light bluish silk
Ribbing—very fine silver tinsel
Silk—white

Back Swimmer Imitations

Back Swimmer Nymph   (Bill Blades)

Wing cases—mottled brown turkey section
Thorax—grey rabbit dubbing
Abdomen—rabbit fur dubbing mixed with a little orange wool
Ribbing—dark brown cotton thread
Legs—brown trimmed hackle bent and lacquered
Silk—brown

Adult Back Swimmer   (Bill Blades)

Wings—mottled brown turkey tied tentlike over body
Thorax—rabbit fur dubbing
Abdomen—rabbit fur and orange wool mixed
Legs—brown hackle bent, trimmed and lacquered
Silk—brown

Scud and Sow Bug Imitations

Fresh-Water Shrimp

Legs—pale olive-grey hackle tied palmer
Body—yellow silk, top and side hackle bound down under ribbing
Ribbing—olive silk
Tail—one pale olive-grey hackle tip
Silk—olive

Grey Sow Bug

Legs—bluish grey dun tied palmer, trimmed off on belly and back
Abdomen—rabbit fur and olive wool mixed
Silk—white

Ant Imitations

Black Ant

Thorax—black silk under lacquer
Body—black silk under lacquer
Legs—black hackle tied sparse between body and thorax
Silk—black

Red Ant

Thorax—orange silk under lacquer
Body—orange silk under lacquer
Legs—light brown hackle tied sparse between body and thorax
Silk—orange

Black Flying Ant

Thorax—black silk under lacquer
Body—black silk under lacquer
Wings—white hackle points tied at sides along body
Legs—black hackle tied sparse between thorax and body
Silk—black

Red Flying Ant

Thorax—orange silk under lacquer
Body—orange silk under lacquer
Wings—bluish grey hackle points tied at sides along body
Legs—light brown hackle tied sparse between thorax and body
Silk—orange

Beetle Imitations

Brown Beetle

Wings—dark brown feather section tied with wing case over whole body
Legs—dark furnace hackle
Body—peacock herl

Black Beetle

Wings—black duck section tied with wing case over whole body
Legs—black hackle
Body—peacock herl

Grasshopper Imitation

Michigan Hopper

Wings—brown mottled turkey around hackle
Hackle—brown and chinchilla mixed and palmer tied, trimmed on sides
Body—red fox fur and yellow wool dubbing
Tails—red-dyed hackle fibers
Egg Sac—red fox and yellow wool mixed dubbing in a loop over tail
Silk—rusty orange

GENERAL BIBLIOGRAPHY

Atherton, John. *The Fly and the Fish.* New York: Macmillan, 1951.

Bergman, Ray. *Just Fishing.* New York: Knopf, 1932.

———. *Trout.* New York: Knopf, 1938; 2nd edition, same, 1952.

Betten, Cornelius. "The Caddis Flies or Trichoptera of New York State." New York State Museum Bulletin No. 292, Albany, 1934.

———. Trichoptera; in "Aquatic Insects in the Adirondacks." New York State Museum Bulletin No. 47. Albany, 1901.

Blades, William F. *Fishing Flies and Fly Tying.* Harrisburg, Pa.: Stackpole, 1951.

Claassen, Peter W. *Plecoptera Nymphs of America (North of Mexico).* Vol. III, Thomas Say Foundation. Springfield, Ill.: Thomas, 1931.

Comstock, J. H. *An Introduction to Entomology,* 2nd edition. Ithaca, N. Y.: Comstock, 1925.

Cross, Reuben R. *Fur, Feathers and Steel.* New York: Dodd, Mead, 1940.

———. *The Complete Fly-Tyer.* New York: Dodd, Mead, 1950.

Davis, K. C. "Sialididae of North and South America." New York State Museum Bulletin No. 68. Albany, 1903.

Flick, Art. *Streamside Guide to Naturals and Their Imitations.* New York: Putnam's, 1947.

Gordon, Theodore. *The Complete Fly Fisherman.* The notes and letters of Theodore Gordon, edited by John McDonald, New York: Scribner's, 1947.

Grove, Alvin R., Jr. *The Lure and Lore of Trout Fishing.* Harrisburg: Stackpole, 1951.

Haig-Brown, Roderick. "Izaak Walton—His Friends and his Rivers." *Field & Stream.* Vol. 58 No. 1. May, 1953.

Hazzard, A. S. "Theories Can't Catch Trout." *Outdoor Life,* Vol. 106 No. 4. October, 1950.

Heacox, Cecil. "The Compleat Life." *Field & Stream,* Vol. 58 No. 1. May, 1953.

Hewitt, Edward Ringwood. *Telling on the Trout.* New York: Scribner's, 1926.

———. *A Trout and Salmon Fisherman for Seventy-Five Years.* New York: Scribner's, 1948.

Hills, John Waller. *A History of Fly Fishing for Trout.* London: Allan, 1921.

Jennings, Preston J. *A Book of Trout Flies.* New York: Derrydale, 1935; Crown, 1948.

Johannsen, O. A. "Aquatic Nematocerous Diptera." New York State Museum Bulletin No. 68. Albany, 1903.

———. "Aquatic Nematocerous Diptera II." New York State Museum Bulletin No. 86. Albany, 1905.

———. "New North American Chironomidae." New York State Museum Bulletin No. 124. Albany, 1908.

———. "Aquatic Diptera." Ithaca, N. Y.: Cornell University Agricultural Experiment Station Memoirs. Pt. I, 1934; Pt. II, 1935; Pt. III, 1937.

Jordan, David Starr, and Evermann, Barton Warren. *American Food and Game Fishes.* New York: Doubleday, 1902.

La Branche, George M. L. *The Dry Fly and Fast Water.* New York: Scribner's, 1914.

Leonard, J. Edson. *Flies.* New York: Barnes, 1950.

Marinaro, Vincent C. *A Modern Dry-Fly Code.* New York: Putnam's, 1950.

Miall, L. C. *Natural History of Aquatic Insects.* New York: Macmillan, 1912.

Michael, William W. *Dry-Fly Trout Fishing.* New York: McGraw-Hill, 1951.

Milne, L. J. "Studies in North American Trichoptera." Privately published. Cambridge, Mass., 1934.

Morgan, Ann Haven. *Field Book of Ponds and Streams.* New York: Putnam's, 1930.

Murphy, E. "Notes on the Biology of our North American Species of Mayflies." Lloyd Library Series Bulletin, Entomological Series No. 2. Cincinnati, O., 1921.

Needham, James G. "Ephemeridae." New York State Museum Bulletin No. 86. Albany, 1905.

————. Plecoptera; in "Aquatic Insects in the Adirondacks." New York State Museum Bulletin No. 47. Albany, 1901.

————. Ephemerida; in "Aquatic Insects in the Adirondacks." New York State Museum Bulletin No. 47. Albany, 1901.

————. "Burrowing Mayflies of our Larger Lakes and Streams." Bureau of Fisheries Bulletin, Vol. 36: 265–292. 1920.

————. Neuroptera; in "Aquatic Insects in the Adirondacks." New York State Museum Bulletin No. 47. Albany, 1901.

Needham, James G., and Lloyd, J. T.   *Life of Inland Waters.* Ithaca, N. Y.: Comstock, 1916.

Needham, James G., and Needham, Paul R.   *A Guide to the Study of Fresh-Water Biology.* New York: American Viewpoint Society, 1927.

Needham, James G., Traver, J. R., and Hsu, Yin-Chi.   *Biology of Mayflies.* Ithaca, N. Y.: Comstock, 1935.

Needham, Paul R.   *Trout Streams.* Ithaca, N. Y.: Comstock, 1938.

————. "The Mortality of Trout." *Scientific American,* Vol. 188 No. 5. May, 1953.

Ovington, Ray.   *How to Take Trout on Wet Flies and Nymphs.* Boston: Little, Brown, 1951.

Schaldach, William J.   *Currents & Eddies.* New York: Barnes, 1944.

Skues, G. E. M.   *The Way of a Trout with a Fly.* London: A. & C. Black, 1921.

Smedley, Harold Hinsdill.   *Fly Patterns and Their Origins.* Muskegon, Mich.: Westshore, 1944.

Steel, Frank R.   *Fly Fishing.* Chicago: Paul, Richmond, 1946; New York: Crown, 1949.

Walton, Izaak.   *The Compleat Angler.* London: Rich, Marriot, 1653.

Ward, H. B., and Whipple, G. C.   *Fresh-Water Biology.* New York: Wiley, 1918.

Wetzel, Charles M.   *Practical Fly Fishing.* Boston: Christopher, 1943.

INDEX

Page numbers of illustrations are given in italics.
Color plates are listed according to the pages they face.

215